PETERBOROUGH FIRST RAILWAY
Yarwell to Peterborough

PETER J. WASZAK, M.Sc.
JOHN W. GINNS

FRONT COVER PICTURE:

The Harwich-Birmingham "Harwich Express" hauled by
Jubilee Class 4-4-0 No 1932 *Anson* passing through Wansford Station in 1904/5
Photo: Canon A J S Freeman Collection

NENE VALLEY RAILWAY
REGISTERED CHARITY No 263617

Published in Great Britain 1995
by Nene Valley Railway Ltd.
Registered Charity No 263617

Compiled and Edited:
Bernard V Cole

All rights reserved. No parts of this book may be reproduced
or transmitted in any form or by any means, electronic, mechanical,
including photocopying, recording or by any information storage and
retrieval system, without the prior permission of the copyright owners
and the Publisher.

ISBN 0 9516980 4 4

Printed by Starprint, Ramsey, Cambs. Tel: (01487) 710977
Typesetting by A.E.S., Ramsey St. Mary's, Cambs. Tel: (01733) 844412
Reproduction by Final Reproductions Ltd, Sawtry, Cambs. Tel: (01487) 830021

FOREWORD

by David Smith
President – Nene Valley Railway

I am delighted that the Nene Valley Railway is the first major Preserved Railway to celebrate the 150th Anniversary of its construction and opening. It is also pleasing that a group of the Society's members have been able to pursue one of the objects of our Charitable Company, to "further the study of, and research into, railways, engines and the building and operation thereof...", by the production of this book.

As a Chartered Surveyor, the history of the line came to life for me when our Solicitors handed over the thick bundle of Deeds from the 1840s with their copperplate hand-written Indentures and Conveyances on parchment, with the names of Peterborough and London Lawyers, one or two of whom were firms known to me personally. I remain full of admiration for the Surveyors and Valuers to the London & Birmingham Railway, who had to locate the owners and then negotiate for the purchase of 390 parcels of land for the building of our stretch of line.

Like so many of my generation, I admit to having been a trainspotter, when a schoolboy, but although I had an Ian Allan *ABC of LMS Locomotives*, my personal knowledge of the old Nene Valley Line, when working, is limited. I must have seen the eastern end of the line in 1939 and when visiting Northampton (Castle) Station in 1944; I probably noted the numbers of locomotives departing for Peterborough. My first clear memory of a train on what is now the NVR, however, was in 1963 when, on a visit to Wansford that autumn, we waited at the level crossing gates for a 'Black 5', on a Northampton passenger service to pass. I did however defy doctor's orders to travel on the last passenger train to Oundle, which the Society organised in 1972.

As President of the Nene Valley Railway and a Past Chairman of the Society, I am sure that this book will provide a worthy record of the early days of our Line, and of its service to the community, in the first 150 years of its life.

PREFACE

When first suggested, this book was seen as being a compilation of articles that had appeared in various issues of *Nene Steam*, the magazine of the Nene Valley Railway. This proved possible with the chapter entitled 'Countdown' which is an edited version of John Ginns' series of 'Countdown 150' articles that appeared in successive issues of *Nene Steam* between the Winter of 1992/93 and Spring 1995. However, with the articles written by Peter Waszak on the various railway sites between Yarwell and Woodstone this was not always possible as much new information has come to light since the articles first appeared in the earlier issues of *Nene Steam*. This additional information, which has greatly added to the knowledge of this part of the Northampton and Peterborough Railway, has come from various sources. Important amongst these have been the original land purchase Deeds which the Nene Valley Railway have had access to following their acquisition of the freehold of the line in early 1994. Duncan Hallam is to be thanked for his considerable assistance in the interpretation of the archaic legal language of the hand-written Deeds. The chapter on Peterborough Station, perhaps better remembered as Peterborough East, is based on material in Peter Waszak's book *Rail Centres: Peterborough* published in 1984 by Ian Allan Ltd who are thanked for permission to use their book as a source of information.

There are many people to be acknowledged and thanked for the help and information they provided either when the original articles were being prepared or were updated. These include G D Austin, Michael Back (Signalling Record Society), Alan Cleaver, Don Crick, D L Franks, E S George, Walter Gilby, Mrs Graham, R H N Hardy, Richard Havergal, Tom Heugh, Roger Manns, Graham Martin, Neil McGregor, Eric Neve, P F Newell, Nick Pigott, J H Price, J Rhodes, B Robinson, Keith Rogers, Albert Spicer, Dr Taylor (Historical Railway Society), Ray Townsin, Neil Vann, Frank Waters, Brian White and Mr Winter (senior). It is quite possible that some names that should have appeared here have not done so simply due to my not knowing of their contribution and to any such I offer my apologies.

Bernard Cole,
April 1995

Chapter One
INTRODUCTION

Standing beside the East Coast Main Line from London to Edinburgh at Peterborough today it is not apparent that this direct route from London was not the first railway to arrive in Peterborough. The Great Northern Railway (GNR) which built the London to York portion of the East Coast Main Line did not open its first section of line from Peterborough, and that a loop line to Lincoln, until October 1848 and the London to Peterborough section was not opened to the public until 5th August, 1850. This was five years after the first railway had arrived in Peterborough, that first railway being the Northampton and Peterborough Railway.

The Northampton and Peterborough Railway (N&PR) was not an independent railway as such but a branch line built by the London and Birmingham Railway Company (L&BR). The branch left the L&BR's main line at a new Blisworth station and ran via Northampton, Thrapston, Oundle and Wansford to Peterborough. It was sanctioned by an Act of Parliament in July 1843 and opened to the public on 2nd June, 1845 though goods traffic did not commence until 15th December, 1845. In Peterborough the N&PR did not have its own station using instead the station being built by the Eastern Counties Railway (ECR) for its branch line from Ely; the ECR later became part of the Great Eastern Railway (GER). The route from Northampton to Peterborough was an easy one, following the valley of the River Nene, and as a consequence the railway has often been referred to as the Nene Valley line. With the only major undertakings being Wansford tunnel and the nearby river bridges, the line was built in little more than a year at a cost of £429,409 (about £9,000 per mile), a remarkably low figure for that period.

At the time of opening the N&PR was one of the first lines in the country to be equipped with electric telegraph apparatus which, despite the initial cost, resulted in numerous operating advantages especially as it was then a single-line railway. Fortunately the N&PR Bill had been amended in March 1843 during its progress through Parliament to authorise a second line of rails, which no doubt resulted in the L&BR purchasing enough land to enable the line to be doubled and constructing the various structures on the railway so as to be able to accommodate such a second line. Within months of opening, traffic was so heavy that this second line was needed; it was subsequently added and in use well before the end of 1846. In that year the L&BR, and of course its line to Peterborough, amalgamated with other railway companies to form the London and North Western Railway (L&NWR).

The opening of three other railway lines had a direct influence on the Nene Valley line. The first of these occurred in 1867 when Wansford, also known locally in the early days as Sibson, became a junction with the opening of the Sibson Extension of the Stamford and Essendine Railway (S&ER). This was a single-track line which ran from Stamford and joined the L&NWR line 80 yards east of Wansford Station. Although initially an independent railway it was at times operated, and later acquired, by the GNR. The Sibson Extension, sometimes referred to as the Wansford branch, survived until 1st June, 1929.

Before the late 1870s the Nene Valley line provided an indirect route between Peterborough, Birmingham and the Midlands which required a reversal at Blisworth. Such a cross-country journey was tortuous, inconvenient and time consuming resulting in a 100-mile journey by the L&NWR route which was both longer and slower than the competing Midland Railway (MR) route via Leicester. On 1st November, 1879 the L&NWR opened its 11-mile connecting line from Yarwell Junction (to the west of Wansford) to Seaton on the Rugby and Stamford Railway which was also part of the L&NWR network. The resulting Peterborough to Rugby line was then developed as a secondary main line, linking Yarmouth and Peterborough to Birmingham, North Wales and Ireland.

The third line was the one and three quarter mile Fletton Loop opened in 1883. This loop line, which ran from the GNR's main line at Fletton Junction to the Nene Valley line at Longville Junction, enabled GNR trains to run from its station in Peterborough to Leicester (Belgrave Road) via Rockingham, Medbourne and Lowesby Junction, and also gave access to Market Harborough and Melton Mowbray. Passenger services (sometimes hauled by Patrick Stirling's famous 2-2-2 locomotives with one pair of 8ft driving wheels) ended in 1916, but the loop was retained for access to local brickyards while sugar-beet traffic continued to use part of the loop until 1991. Longville Junction was taken out in 1929 leaving Fletton Junction as the only connection, reinstated in 1947 and taken out again about 1961.

With the outbreak of the First World War in 1914 the railways came under government control with the Nene Valley line forming an important link in a secondary cross-country route. Military traffic increased along the line though there was a curtailment of unnecessary passenger services. Following the cessation of hostilities the railways returned to the control of their individual companies but as a result of the Railways Act, 1921 these companies were grouped into four main groups as from 1st January, 1923. With grouping the L&NWR and its Nene Valley line became part of the London Midland and Scottish Railway (LM&SR) while the GNR, which controlled the Stamford-Wansford branch and the Fletton Loop, and the GER, which owned the Peterborough station used by the Nene Valley line, became part of the London and North Eastern Railway (L&NER).

On 1st September, 1939, two days before the Second World War was declared, the railways were again placed under government direction with operating controls being introduced to make the most effective use of the railways. As in the First World War, non-essential passenger services were curtailed with priority being given to the movement of the armed forces, war materials and munitions. The Nene Valley line again became part of a secondary cross-country route and saw the busiest time it was ever to experience. After the war the railway companies regained control of their lines, but not for long, as the railways were nationalised on 1st January, 1948 to form British Railways (BR). The Nene Valley line became part of BR's London Midland Region (LMR) while the L&NER's lines in the Peterborough area became part of the Eastern Region (ER).

Following nationalisation changes were few at first. However, in the 1950s and 1960s came a period of rationalisation. Traffic and services declined as passengers took to car and coach travel while goods were increasingly conveyed by lorry. Stations closed – Orton Waterville in 1942 and Castor and Wansford in 1957. Passenger trains between Peterborough and Northampton ceased on 2nd May, 1964, and through freight traffic was discontinued from 10th April, 1965. A limited freight and special train service was retained to Oundle from the Peterborough direction with the line being downgraded and suffering the inevitable reductions in track work. On the Peterborough to Rugby line the passenger service and through freight traffic ended on 6th June, 1966. From 26th February, 1967 the line between Peterborough and Wansford was worked as a single line thus reverting to the situation which existed when the Nene Valley line opened in 1845.

The Nene Valley line's main surviving traffic was ironstone from Nassington Quarries to the west of Wansford on the former Rugby line with this service ceasing in December 1970. Following this the line only provided the connection to Oundle, its thrice weekly goods service and occasional Oundle School Special ceasing in 1972. In November of that year BR closed the line completely and following closure the track east of Longueville Junction, together with most of the ballast, was removed. With that the one hundred and twenty years' story of the Northampton and Peterborough Railway came to an end.

One chapter in the line's history had now closed but another was about to begin.

This book is not a history of the whole of what started as the Northampton and Peterborough Railway but of that portion of the line from Yarwell to Peterborough which has survived into preservation as the Nene Valley Railway. However, in setting the scene for the railway's conception, construction and opening, the next chapter will look in addition at events which occurred outside that eastern portion of the line.

Chapter Two
COUNTDOWN

Before the opening of the Northampton and Peterborough Railway life along the Nene Valley had never travelled any faster than a person could walk or a horse could gallop. Although the 19th century had brought improvements to the turnpike roads and in the Nene navigation, 10 miles per hour was still about the fastest anyone could hope to travel.

By early 1842 things had been happening elsewhere that would eventually bring about untold changes to the Nene Valley, but apart from rumours and gossip it is unlikely the local folk could have grasped the significance of these events. The London and Birmingham Railway was open and those from Northampton who could afford it could catch a coach to 'the Northampton Station' at Blisworth and be in London in just two and a half hours. There were also ambitious plans for a direct railway line from London, via Peterborough to York. Peterborough was rapidly becoming a focus of railway attention.

Since 1838 a Northampton delegation had been unsuccessfully lobbying the London and Birmingham Directors for a branch line to Northampton. In May 1842, however, the Directors at last agreed to construct a new Blisworth station (actually nearer to Gayton) at a site more suitable for a junction for a line to Northampton and beyond. The extent to which their decision was influenced by the Northampton delegation or by the prospects of heading off the competition at the Great North Road (at Wansford) and at Peterborough is still open to conjecture.

This chapter looks at the events leading up to the construction and opening of the Northampton and Peterborough Railway from contemporary minutes and newspaper reports in the manner and language as they appeared at that time.

IN THE BEGINNING...
Friday, 11th November, 1842

The L&BR Co Directors meet. Minute 2126: It is resolved *"That a branch railway connecting Peterborough, the intermediate towns and places and the adjoining districts with the London and Birmingham Line near Gayton, would conduce to the public accommodation and the particular interests of this Company..."*

Wednesday, 16th November, 1842

A meeting of interested parties is held in Northampton, Mr Stephenson being present. It is stated by the Parliamentary Agent and also by Mr Creed, Secretary, L&BR Company, *"that unless the line could be performed at a very moderate expense, and receive encouragement from the several towns near which it passed, it could not be carried out"*.

Friday, 18th November, 1842

A public meeting is held at Wellingborough Town Hall. The public give their unanimous support for the railway.

Tuesday, 22nd November, 1842
A public meeting is held at the White Hart, Thrapston. Wide approval is given for the railway.

Saturday, 26th November, 1842
The *Northampton Herald* carries an Editorial questioning the motives of the Railway Company...

Monday, 28th November, 1842
A meeting is held at the Guildhall, Northampton. Public approval is expressed.

Wednesday, 7th December, 1842
Public approval is expressed at a meeting in Peterborough.

Friday, 9th December, 1842
L&BR Directors read the report from the Blisworth/Peterborough Committee including a report by Major-General C W Pasley, Inspector-General of Railways.

Saturday, 10th December, 1842
Editorial in the *Northampton Herald* refers to widespread public approval but opposition from landowners – *"excessive compensation to these gentry will inevitably result in higher fares"*.

Tuesday, 13th December, 1842
Another public meeting is held at the White Hart Hotel, Thrapston. The public expressed its wish for the support of the landowners.

Wednesday, 14th December, 1842
A public meeting is held at the Talbot Hotel, Oundle. Unanimous support and request for approval to be sought from landowners.

Thursday, 15th December, 1842
A meeting of landowners is held at the White Hart Hotel, Thrapston, Earl Filtzwilliam in the Chair. The *Northampton Herald* reporter is observed in the meeting, but after questioning is allowed to remain.
Mr Bouverie and Mr Smyth each complain that the first they knew of the railway was on seeing *"a gentleman placing flags in his field"*. Other objections are expressed and it cannot have passed unnoticed that someone present states that on other railways 50% above normal prices has been paid for some land!

Saturday, 24th December, 1842
The *Herald* reports on a letter of opposition from Stamford, which was the result of the railway not passing through that town.

Saturday, 31st December, 1842
The *Northampton Mercury* reports on a public meeting at Spalding, seeking support for the railway.
Over 150 attend a public meeting at Bourne. Both support for, and opposition to, the railway are expressed. Amongst the objections is the claim that *"...if built, the line from Blisworth would impede the construction of the line from Cambridge"*.
M H H Filton, Engineer for the Nene Commissioners, asserts that the Syston to Peterborough route is preferable as it *"would, unlike the Northampton and Peterborough Line, have no navigation to compete with"*.

Friday, 6th January, 1843
The *Stamford Mercury* carries an Editorial referring to the proposed railway *"...to the admiration of the many and the annoyance of the few..."* and mentions the proposed route through a tunnel, a station at Wansford and the site of the station at Peterborough, etc...

Monday, 9th January, 1843
A meeting is held of the Trustees of the Peterborough and Wellingborough Turnpike Road, at the Talbot Hotel, Oundle, *"for the purpose of taking into consideration... the proposed line of railway from Northampton to Peterborough crossing the line of road in various places..."*

Thursday, 12th January, 1843
A public meeting is held at the Chequers Inn, Holbeach, to consider the proposed railway. A resolution is passed, *"that this meeting hereby gives unqualified support to the measure..."*

Friday, 13th January, 1843
L&BR Directors meet. The tender of Messrs. Gressel & Peto for construction of the line is tabled. It is resolved *"that in the opinion of the Board... the works of the Northampton and Peterborough branch should be offered to contractors (to be named) in either two parts or as a whole, the rails and stations being reserved, etc..."*

Saturday, 14th January, 1843
The *Northampton Herald* reports on a letter from Thos Motley, Civil Engineer, proposing a horse-operated railway from Northampton to Peterborough at 10 mph instead of 20 mph.

Monday, 16th January, 1843
L&BR Directors meet; cost of construction of Peterborough branch estimated at £500,000 but the line forecast to be *"not of a profitable character"*.
It was resolved to apply to Parliament for the authority to build the line.

Thursday, 19th January, 1843
Public meeting at the Sessions House, Wisbech. General approval for the railway and the Members of Parliament for that county to be respectfully asked to support the Bill in Parliament. The meeting is of the opinion that sufficient land should be purchased to enable the track to be doubled when the traffic calls for such.
The *Stamford Mercury* reports a letter from Lynn Corporation in favour of the railway.

Tuesday, 24th January, 1843
Another public meeting is held at Thrapston and approval is re-affirmed.

Wednesday, 25th January, 1843
Landowners meet again at Thrapston...
Also on the same day: Extraordinary Meeting of the Nene Commissioners (Eastern Division) at the Talbot Inn, Oundle *"to consider assent, dissent or neutrality re the proposed railway..."*

Thursday, 26th January, 1843
Adjourned meeting (from December 31st) is held at Bourne. Approval given for the line from Blisworth and local MPs from Lords and Commons be instructed to support the Bill.

Friday, 27th January, 1843
Stamford Mercury reports on public approval to the L&BR's intention to apply for an act *"in the coming Session... for a railway from Blisworth to this city (Peterborough).*
"Reports are circulated that Earl Fitzwilliam and his friends are opposed to the intended line but we cannot for a moment suppose that His Lordship will stand in opposition to the wishes of the people of Peterborough..."

Saturday, 4th February, 1843
Editorial in the *Northampton Mercury* expressing concern at the interference to traffic to be expected from the level crossing in Bridge Street, Northampton.

Cambridge Chronicle Editorial opposing the railway: *"It will ruin us without enriching them"*. Locals are urged to call upon their MPs to oppose the Bill.

Saturday, 11th February, 1843

Cambridge Chronicle prints a letter from an 'Anti-Monopolist' claiming that *"the most exaggerated statements have been issued by the London & Birmingham Company for the sake of making out a good cause"*.

Friday, 17th February, 1843

First Sitting of Commons Committee on petitions for/against the Northampton & Peterborough Bill. After some delays on procedures Mr George Parker Bidder, Engineer for the proposed line, confirms that the details shown on the tabled plans are in order. Many details are discussed and it is revealed that some 1400-1500 different properties will be interfered with by the railway.

Tuesday, 28th February, 1843

First Reading of the Bill in the House of Commons. For: 94 Against: 80.

Tuesday, 7th March, 1843

Second Reading of the Bill in the Commons. For: 94 Against: 80. The 'considerable opposition' is reported by the *Northampton Mercury*.

Friday, 10th March, 1843

L&BR Directors meet. In response to Opposition claims that the proposed single line poses a risk to public safety a Clause is to be added to the Bill authorising a second line of rails should this be deemed necessary.

It is also resolved that *"should it be deemed important to neutralise the opposition of the town of Stamford, the Committee be empowered to make the Line stop short of Peterborough"*.

However, if the level crossings are not allowed the Bill is to be withdrawn.

Monday, 20th March, 1843

The Northampton & Peterborough Bill goes before the House of Commons Committee. A great many witnesses and much evidence is heard. Supporting the railway the Rev Peter William Pegus, farmer of Uffington House near Stamford, for example, claims that *"all the best cattle and sheep go by road to London – cattle take six or seven days, sheep take 10 days – with considerable losses in price"*. This claim is confirmed the following day, in Committee, by Mr Thomas Slater of Kensington, Butcher to Her Majesty and the London Nobility. Mr Slater agrees that considerable losses in cattle and sheep prices are caused by the long road journeys.

Saturday, 25th March, 1843

Cambridge Chronicle reports on opposition at a public meeting at Cambridge. Many criticisms are levelled at the proposal including the allegations that the Line *"was to travel over a very low swampy district nearly always subjected to protracted inundation"*.

Friday, 7th April, 1843

L&BR Directors meet. Considerable concern is expressed at attempts by the Opposition to delay the Third Reading of the Bill until after Easter. The need for continual canvassing of certain Members is emphasised to counter the *"formidable opposition"* expected.

Tuesday, 9th May, 1843

Third Reading of the Bill in the Commons. For: 195 Against: 164.

Monday, 15th May, 1843

First Reading of the Bill in the House of Lords. On that day the *Northampton Mercury* urges townsfolk to sign a petition at the Town Hall, in favour of the Bill.

Tuesday, 23rd May, 1843
The *Mercury* reports that a petition from the merchants and inhabitants of Great Yarmouth is presented to the House of Lords, in favour of the Bill.
Northampton Town Council agree to petition the Lords in favour of the Bill.
Friday, 26th May, 1843
The Bishop of Peterborough presents a petition to the Lords supporting the Bill. A petition in favour of the Bill is also presented to the Lords by the Duke of Cleveland, on behalf of the City of Norwich.
Thursday, 1st June, 1843
Second Reading of the Bill in the House of Lords. For: 52 Against: 51.
Wednesday, 21st June, 1843
The Bill passes the House of Lords Committee.
Monday, 26th June, 1843
The Bill is read and passed a third time in the House of Lords.
Tuesday, 4th July, 1843
The Northampton and Peterborough Railway Bill receives the Royal Assent.
Thursday, 27th July, 1843
Mr Stephenson anbd Mr Bidder attend a dinner at the Angel Hotel, Northampton, to celebrate the passing of the Bill.

IRON AND SLEEPERS
Friday, 14th July, 1843
L&BR Co Directors meet at Euston. Following the Chairman's report that the Northampton and Peterborough Railway Bill has received the Royal Assent, it is resolved (Minute 2311) that a Committee consisting of:

The Chairman	Capt Moorsom
The Deputy Chairman	Mr Prevost
Mr Boothby	Mr Smith
Mr Cropper	Mr Walker

be appointed to direct and superintend the necessary measures connected with the construction of the Railway.

A report is then read from Mr Stephenson, 12th inst, on the measures necessary to undertake forthwith, and making an offer to provide resident engineers, inspectors, drawings and specifications for a fixed sum.

Minute 2312: It is ordered that the Report be referred to the Committee and that they be instructed to enquire whether it may not be expedient that contracts be made forthwith for the iron and sleepers required for the permanent way, and to undertake measures accordingly.

It is also ordered that immediate steps be taken for setting out the line and for obtaining possession of the land required for the Railway. A note in the Directors' Minutes at this stage states that the business of the Northampton and Peterborough Railway is now transferred to the Northampton and Peterborough Committee.

Wednesday, 26th July, 1843
The Northampton and Peterborough (N&P) Committee meets for the first time. After reading Minute 2311 of the Board, appointing the Committee, it is agreed that Mr Stephenson be requested to undertake responsibility for the engineering works of the Line, his remuneration to be contingent on the completion of the works within his estimate of £370,000. This estimate does not include stations, land and extras such as wagon turntables which are considered to be part of the stations.

It is resolved that Mr Stephenson be instructed to proceed forthwith in setting out the Line as approved in the Bill, and to survey that part of the Line with reference to the letter received from Earl Fitzwilliam. *(This presumably refers to the Earl's proposed deviation to take the Line on a more southerly route via Kate's Cabin and Alwalton thus further away from his Milton Hall residence – JWG)*

It is ordered that Mr Stephenson be instructed to prepare specifications for the rails and sleepers required for the Line, the former to be of the weight and section of the London and Birmingham rails, and to be delivered at London, Birmingham, Rugby, Wolverton or Peterborough, the whole or portions thereof, and to be contracted for as may be deemed expedient.

It is agreed that application be made to Mr Francis Sanders of Derby, requesting him to undertake valuation of the land required for the Line.

Friday, 11th August, 1843

N&P Committee meets. Mr Stephenson's specifications for contracts for rails and sleepers is read and approved and it is resolved that the same be advertised and a copy of the advertisement sent to the principal iron-masters in Wales.

Monday, 28th August, 1843

Advertisement appears in *Aris's Birmingham Gazette* (one of the many newspapers to carry this advertisement) inviting tenders for the supply of 6600 tons of rails for the Northampton and Peterborough Railway; the rails to be parallel (*i.e. 'double-headed' – JWG*) and of the form adopted on the London and Birmingham Railway, and weighing 75 lbs to the yard.

Wednesday, 30th August, 1843

At a special meeting of the N&P Committee Mr Stephenson formally agrees to accept responsibility for the engineering work of the Line.

Saturday, 2nd September, 1843

The *Northampton Mercury* carries an advertisement inviting tenders for the supply of 80,000 timber sleepers for the Line, nominally 10" x 5" x 9'0" long if rectangular, or not less than 10" x 6" at the narrow end if round in section. Delivery of sleepers to be completed by June 1st, 1844.

Thursday, 7th September, 1843

N&P Committee meets. It is proposed that the terms proposed by Mr Sanders for his services in purchasing the land required for the Line be approved. His remuneration is to be £1,000 subject to the land costing the estimated £100,000. Noted in the Minutes (written in pencil in the left-hand border) is the estimated cost of the Line:

Land and compensation	£100,000
Iron	£ 33,000
Sleepers	£ 17,000
Works	£190,000
Engineering, to Mr Stephenson	£ 10,000
Surveying	£ 1,000
Parliamentary Bill	£ 15,000
	£366,000
plus stations, etc. in total:	£500,000

Mr Bidder then presents his report giving details of the proposed alternative route through Earl Fitzwilliam's Estate at Alwalton, and the line proposed by His Lordship. It is resolved (Minute 12) that the Committee, although sincerely desirous of meeting

His Lordship's views... in consideration of the additional expenses... cannot adopt the line he has suggested nor even the intermediate line which is marked on the plan under their existing legal powers of their Act, and in addition to this paramount objection, they are apprehensive that the greatly increased accumulation of spoil banks which must result from the proposed deviation from the Parliamentary Line would be a serious objection to the neighbourhood.

The Notices of Contracts for rails and sleepers to be tendered for this day are tabled. The tenders are opened and examined. It is resolved (Minute 13) that the tender of the Rhymney Iron Company to supply 6,600 tons of malleable iron rails, conformable to specifications, at £5 17s 0d per ton delivered in London and at £6 0s 0d per ton delivered in Wisbech, be accepted.

It is resolved (Minute 14) that the following tenders for sleepers be accepted:
Thos. Jackson – 15,000 natural grown Scotch Fir at 3/11½ each, delivered on the Line.
John Cameron – 30,000 Fir and Larch, not fewer than a quarter natural grown at 3/6 each.
George Vertue – 35,000 Fir and Larch at 4/5½ each.

It is resolved (Minute 15) that the form of Contract for tenders for chairs be approved. *(Did Mr Bidder remind the Committee that chairs would also be needed? – JWG)*

Friday, 15th September and **Monday, 18th September, 1843**

Advertisements inviting tenders for the supply of chairs for the Line appear in the *Stamford Mercury* and in *Aris's Birmingham Gazette* respectively – any quantity not exceeding 1400 tons, of the form used on the main London to Birmingham Line: joint chair to weigh 25 lbs; intermediate chair to weigh 23 lbs.

Wednesday, 20th September, 1843

N&P Committee meets. A letter is read from Earl Fitzwilliam, in response to Minute 12 of 7th September. (No detail recorded)

Tenders from 26 Iron Masters are tabled, for the supply of chairs required for the Line. It is resolved (Minute 16) that the tender of Mr George H Barrow for the supply of 1400 tons of chairs according to pattern and specification, and delivered in Birmingham at the price of £3 19s 0d per ton be accepted.

CONTRACTS FOR WORKS

Friday, 13th October, 1843

N&P Committee of the L&BR Co meets. Various items of business are minuted including further correspondence from Earl Fitzwilliam, which is referred to Mr Stephenson and Mr Bidder. Payments totalling £13,612 0s 11d (in connection with the proposed railway) are reported.

It is resolved to appoint a Finance Sub-Committee consisting of the Chairman, Mr Prevost, Mr Boothby and Mr Young.

Saturday, 14th October, 1843

The *Northampton Mercury* carries an advertisement representing one of the first attempts by local property owners to exploit the impending invasion of railway contractors: a house and cottage at Doddington (near Wellingborough) are offered to let to any contractor upon the Blisworth and Peterborough Railway...

Wednesday, 22nd November, 1843

First meeting of the N&P Finance Sub-Committee. Mr Sanders reports land purchases to date for the Line totalling £21,730 5s 6d in respect of a total land area of 70 acres, 1 rod and 15 poles.

Friday, 24th November and **Saturday, 25th November, 1843**

The *Stamford Mercury* and the *Northampton Mercury*, respectively, carry editorials referring to the construction of Wansford Tunnel. Preparation for the works is expected to start early in the coming year. The tunnelling from the south stonepit to opposite the Ferryboat House will be one of the first steps, and the excellent stone so obtained will be required for bridges and other buildings. Two hundred men, we understand, will be employed on this work until its completion.

Saturday, 25th November and **Friday, 1st December, 1843**

The *Northampton Mercury* and the *Stamford Mercury*, respectively, carry notices concerning tenders for Contracts for Works on the N&PR. The Directors of the L&BR Co will meet at the Euston Station, London, on Thursday, 11th January, 1844, at 12 o'clock, to receive tenders for the construction of the said railway in the following divisions:

Contract No 1 – Blisworth to Wellingborough.

Contract No 2 – Wellingborough to Oundle.

Contract No 3 – Oundle to Peterborough.

Saturday, 9th December, 1843

The *Cambridge Chronicle* reports that a piece of land has been purchased by the L&BR Co near the river, where a quantity of materials for the railroad from Peterborough to Blisworth is already deposited.

Thursday, 14th December, 1843

N&P Committee meets. The form of advertisement for tenders to construct the Line and Works is tabled. It is resolved that the same be approved and inserted in the usual newspapers. *(Although such notices have already appeared in the local papers – JWG)*

An invoice is approved for 232 tons, 14 cwt, 2 qrs and 10 lbs in respect of rails from the Rhymney Iron Co shipped at Newport on board the *Romulus* for Wisbech, and enclosing a Bill of Lading for the same, £1245 2s 1d. It is also resolved that rails are to be insured in the usual way. Other business is discussed including further transactions for land purchases.

Mr Bidder reports that Mr Cameron has commenced the delivery of sleepers under his contract with the Company. *(These presumably being the 'materials' reported by the* Cambridge Chronicle, *December 9th – JWG)*

Friday, 15th December, 1843

The *Stamford Mercury* carries an advertisement to contractors, etc. announcing that Messrs Bennett & Son of Whittlesea have a licence from the Anti Dry Rot Co to use Kyan's Patent for the preservation of timber to be used on the N&PR. Tanks are now ready for saturating the timber and the Works are close to the river for transporting treated timbers to the intended line.

Saturday, 16th December, 1843

According to the *Cambridge Chronicle* the largest ship, 350 tons, berthed at Wisbech today. *(Is this the* Romulus? *– JWG)*

Saturday, 23rd December, 1843

The *Northampton Mercury* reporting on the Railway states that a considerable quantity of materials required in the construction of the Railroad has been deposited at intervals along the line.

Wednesday, 27th December, 1843

N&PR Committee meets to approve further payments for rails, etc and land purchases, averaging £168 0s 0d per acre.

Wednesday, 4th January, 1843

N&PR Committee meets. Further payments are approved, including £887 13s 0d for 166 tons of rails, Rhymney Iron Co, shipped aboard the *Cordelia* for Wisbech. It is reported that land purchases now total £39,475 2s 6d.

Thursday, 11th January, 1844

N&P Committee meets. After introductory formalities concerning the Contracts for Works, tenders from 18 contractors are tabled. The following are accepted:

(Minute 35) Mr John Stephenson of Derby, for Contract No 1, Blisworth to Wellingborough, for the sum of £48,132.

(Minute 36) The same Party, for Contract No 2, Wellingborough to Oundle, for the sum of £64,847.

(Minute 37) Mr John Brogden of Ardwick, near Manchester, for Contract No 3, Oundle to Peterborough, for the sum of £74,810.

The Contracts themselves are documents of considerable complexity. As well as itemising the price of each and every part of the works to be undertaken, the responsibilities and duties of the Contractor, including his treatment of his workmen, are left in no doubt. Contract No 1 runs to 78 pages and Contract No 2 is of similar length. Contract No 3, Oundle to Peterborough, contains 58 pages. The extracts below give some idea of the detailed planning and organisation involving the Railway Company and the Contractor, even before construction begins:

SCOPE OF THE CONTRACT:

- ...between the London and Birmingham Railway Company and John Brogden of Manchester in the County of Palatine of Lancaster, Railway Contractor for constructing the Railway...
- ...from the west side of the road from Oundle to Peterborough... and terminating at the west side of the Fair Field at Peterborough... a distance of 12 miles and 70 chains approximately... for the sum of £74,810.
- John Brogden to find and provide all the requisite materials for the several works (except rails, chairs and sleepers...)
- Completion to be by 31st March, 1845.
- ...to be maintained for one year after opening to the public, by John Brogden...

WORKMEN:

- Wages: Excavators (navvies) 3/3 (16p) per day.
  Bricklayers 5/- (25p) per day.
  Carpenters 4/6 (22p) per day.
  Smiths 5/6 (27p) per day.
  Labourers 3/3 (16p) per day.
  Horse and cart and driver 7/- (35p) per day.
- Workmen to be paid at least every fortnight, at a place to be named by the Railway Company and in the presence of a Company official.
- The men are not to work on Sunday, unless agreed by the Company in the case of emergency.
- No article of consumption to be retailed to the workmen.

WORKS – GENERAL:

- John Brogden to fence work areas.
- John Brogden to dispose of all spoil earth at specified places.
- Spoil not to be tipped in excess of 400 yds from the railway.
- No steam engine or brick-making within 800 yds of a mansion without leave of the owner or occupier.
- The Railway Company to provide 1500 tons of rails and 360 tons of chairs to be delivered at Wisbech. 17,000 wooden sleepers to be delivered at such places along

the banks of the Nene as shall from time to time be fixed. John Brogden to be responsible for transporting the same to points where required.

UNIT PRICES:
- Average price of earthworks deposited in embankments 11¼d (4½p) per cubic yard.
- The same when length of lead does not exceed ¼ mile – 9½d (4p) per cubic yard.
- Excavation for tunnelling, including all contingencies – 3/3 (16p) per cubic yard.
- Soiling and sodding embankments, including sowing with rye grass and clover seed at not less than 3lb of mixture per acre – 2½d (1p) per superficial yard.
- Cast iron in girders – £9 0s 0d per ton.
- Ornamental cast iron work – £10 0s 0d per ton.

PRICES FOR SPECIFIC EARTHWORKS:

Cuttings and embankments are identified by numbers as they occur. Starting at Oundle and proceeding towards Peterborough, 13 separate earthworks are identified in this way. The following examples occur as the proposed line approaches and penetrates the high ground near the south Stone pit:
- Cutting No 5 £979 8s 0d.
- Cutting No 6 £1512 10s 0d.
- Sibson Tunnel £7486 17s 0d.
- Cutting No 7 £3669 10s 0d.
- Cutting No 8 £193 2s 0d.
- Embankment No 9 £363 9s 0d.
- Embankment No 10 £1841 16s 0d.

PRICES FOR SPECIFIC STRUCTURES:

In addition to the earthworks, there are a considerable number of construction works to undertake and details of these are set out on drawings provided by the Railway Company. Here there is some standardisation: the specification of all surface crossings, for example, is given on Drawing No 21.

Proceeding eastwards from the proposed site of the Elton Station, for example:
- Surface crossing, 12 ft, (Drawing No 21) £94 16s 0d.
- Bridge over brook (4) £199 12s 2d.
- Tunnel (7) £15,790 10s 0d.
- Surface crossing, 35 ft, London Road, Sibson, (21) £255 7s 0d.
- Bridge over River Nene (8) £1045 0s 0d.
- Bridge over brook (9) £180 15s 0d.
- Surface crossing, 12 ft, (21) £158 0s 0d.

The above works included cuttings and under bridges for a single line, except for the tunnel and its cuttings which are to be for two lines.

"THEY'VE STARTED ON THE RAILWAY"

Stacks of sleepers and other materials for the new railway are appearing at intervals alongside the Grand Junction Canal between Gayton and Northampton and by the River Nene all the way to Peterborough. There is no formal ceremony, no precise starting date nor particular place, but one day, towards the end of January, somewhere along the Valley, the cry is heard – *"They've started on the railway"*.

Friday 19th January, 1844

The *Stamford Mercury* reports that two houses at Wansford have been taken by a gentleman connected with the Railway. Messrs Wright and Russell, from London, are the sub-contractors for the Peterborough portion, and have been for some days located at Wansford.

Saturday, 20th January, 1844

The *Northampton Mercury* reports that at Wisbech the port is full of shipping bringing in rails, upward of 100 sail being expected in with that article during the spring, which will be a great addition to the Port Harbour dues.

Wednesday, 24th January, 1844

N&P Committee meets. A Bill of Lading of ships arrived at Wisbech is received, involving payment of £2,182 16s 11d to the Rhymney Iron Co A letter is tabled from Mr Hiscox, relating to Freightage of rails for £433 19s 1d. It is reported that land purchases for the Line now total £64,153 6s 6d, including £500 0s 0d for land for the Sibson Tunnel.

Thursday, 25th January, 1844

Work started today on the tunnel at South Stonepit, Wansford, according to the *Stamford Mercury*. Three shafts are to be sunk from which to dig out the tunnel and 136,000 cubic yards of earth are to be removed at each end before stone is reached. It is expected that Mr Jones from Sheffield will have the contract for making the tunnel itself. The men already at work are superintended by Mr Brogden and his agent Mr Pears, Mr Thomas Bartlett of the London and Birmingham Railway Co being in overall charge. There have been numerous tenders from sub-contractors, including one for a large order for wheelbarrows at 10/- (50p) each.

Thursday, 1st February, 1844

The *Stamford Mercury* reports that work began today on sinking the first shaft for the tunnel at Wansford, Mr George Bird from the South-Eastern Railway in Kent being foreman over the men on this work. This week a cut, one spit deep, has been made all the way from the tunnel mouth to Oundle, this marking out the line.

Wednesday, 7th February, 1844

N&P Committee meets. Reported in full is a letter from Mr Stephenson, concerning his instructions for superintending the works. Payments to the contractors are to be made on completion of the works, and not by measurements, thus reducing the work of the Resident Engineers. Mr Bidder is to direct the work on Contract No 2 (Wellingborough to Oundle), but Resident Engineers for Contracts Nos. 1 and 3 have been appointed. Mr Stephenson also states in his letter, *"In addition to these gentlemen I have placed an experienced and trustworthy person at Wisbech to receive and inspect the permanent way materials"*. Sub-Engineers or Inspectors are to be appointed according to the number of separate works put in hand by the contractors, the drawings being all prepared in London.

The Committee also deals today with further rail deliveries, land purchases, etc.

Referring to the work on Wansford tunnel, the *Cambridge Chronicle* reports that today one shaft is now down to 20 ft, the bricklayers having worked all night. The anticipated rock has not been reached, but bad blue clay has been encountered, mixed with small sea shells.

Saturday, 10th February, 1844

The *Northampton Mercury* reports today on the work on Wansford tunnel shafts. In addition to the 40 men presently employed on the tunnel, large numbers are lying about the villages expecting to be engaged.

Tuesday, 13th February, 1844

The miners in one of the shafts sinking at Wansford for the Railway, had a narrow escape from destruction this night, reports the *Stamford Mercury*, when at a depth of 26 ft an immense mass of earth fell in, owing to the action of springs which abound. The men at the mouth of the shaft happening to have their hands on the windlass at the instant the alarm was given, the miners were drawn up; under less providential circumstances they must have lost their lives, for just as they reached the top in the box used for bringing them up, the whole brickwork of the shaft fell in at once. The other shaft remains uninjured, and the brickwork seems to stand well. About 100 men are now employed on the works at Wansford.

Friday, 23rd February, 1844

The *Stamford Mercury* reports that the railway works at Wansford continue without interruption and fresh hands are daily set on, but the number of men who arrive from all parts searching employment greatly exceeds the force required. The roads in consequence have become very dangerous at night. The manager of the works has taken a field of some acres at Yarwell where good clay is found, and brickmaking is to be carried on to a considerable extent.

Wednesday, 28th February, 1844

N&P Committee meets. An invoice is received from the Rhymney Iron Co for £364 15s 0d, with respect to rails shipped aboard the *Hiram* for London. *(Is this considered a better port for delivery of rails required at the Blisworth end of the Line? – JWG)*. Land purchases for the Line reported to now total £88,191 9s 9d.

Thursday, 7th March, 1844

N&P Committee meets. The suggested alteration of the site of the Peterborough station is discussed and it is reported that the inhabitants and the Dean and Chapter (who own most of the land involved) are in favour of the change, but Earl Fitzwilliam, who has a lease of a small piece of land required, is opposed to it.

The L&BR Co Way and Works Committee also meets today. Mr Jackson attends the meeting and requests approval to convey sleepers, which he is contracted to supply for the Peterborough Line, by the ballast trains, free of toll, from Camden station to Blisworth.

Friday, 8th March, 1844

L&BR Co Directors meet. The Minutes of the N&P Committee are received.

There is considerable discussion concerning the Company's response to proposals for rail lines from Cambridge to Lincoln via Peterborough, from Lincoln to Nottingham, and from Boston and Lincoln. It is then resolved that Mr Jackson be permitted to convey his sleepers for the Northampton and Peterboough Line from Camden to Blisworth in his own wagons at a toll of 1d ($\frac{1}{2}$p) per ton mile.

Also today the *Stamford Mercury* carries an Editorial expressing concern that in spite of public approval for the Peterborough station to be sited in Bates Close, closer to the City, Earl Fitzwilliam chooses to object.

Friday, 15th March, 1844

The *Stamford Mercury* reports that last Monday a warrant was obtained by a Peterborough man named Spay against one of the railroad navvies named Whitehead, for an assault. Mr Bristow, Chief Constable, went the same afternoon to execute it, when he was most brutally assaulted by a large party of bankers, banded together to resist his authority, and received a severe wound on the head from a stone. Hare, one of the city police, exerted himself to the upmost to secure the offending parties, but he and Mr Bristow being overpowered by numbers, were obliged to leave the bankers masters of the field.

Application is about to be made for a troop of horse to be stationed at Peterborough during the progress of the railroad works.

Wednesday, 20th March, 1844

N&P Committee meets. It is reported that Earl Fitzwilliam has given notice of his objection to the proposed level crossing at Alwalton *(presumably near Lynch Farm – JWG)* and his intention to apply to the Court of Chancery for an injunction if the work is preceded with. It is resolved that the matter be left in the hands of Mr Parker (the L&BR Company's Solicitor), the Committee not being disposed to involve the Company in a Chancery Suit.

There is some discussion concerning the erection, near Northampton, of a new lock house for the Grand Junction Canal Co, the present lock house becoming the property of the Railway Company. A complaint is received from Lord Montague's solicitor, that the contractor has opened a shop near Oundle for supplying his men with provisions on the Truck system.

A letter is received from Mr Wickens, Clerk to the Magistrates of Northampton, 19th inst, calling attention to the fact of the contractor (Mr J Stephenson) having established the Truck system in that town for supplying his men with provisions. It is ordered that the letter is referred to Mr Parker – and a copy of it to Mr J Stephenson – Mr Parker to be authorised to take measures under the powers of the Contracts for putting an end to these proceedings.

Friday, 22nd March, 1844

The *Stamford Mercury* reports that the works are proceeding rapidly at Wansford; two more shafts for the tunnel have been begun, in the fields of Mr Trayton and Mr Boyall, near the Elton road. The contracts for sinking them have been taken by Messrs Williams and Jones, and Messrs Green and Eno.

The recent wet weather has caused the river level to rise and with it the usual problems of flooding, which must be impeding overall progress of the railway.

Wednesday, 27th March, 1844

N&P Committee meets. A reply is received from Mr J Stephenson, contractor, concerning his alleged use of the Truck system to pay his men. A copy of his letter is to be sent to Mr Wickens, Clerk to the Northampton Borough Council.

Land purchases now total £93,171 15s 3d.

It is ordered that estimates be prepared of the probable cost of erecting a bridge for Earl Fitzwilliam's private road at Alwalton, and of the probable cost of diverting the road at that point, as proposed.

Friday, 29th March, 1844

The *Stamford Mercury* reports the Railway Company has entered into contracts with three surgeons between Northampton and Peterborough to attend the labouring bankers during the works on that line, at the sum of £70 per annum each surgeon. Mr Clapham of Wansford has taken one of the contracts.

The *Mercury* also reports that the making of bricks for the works at Wansford is proceeding rapidly, good clay for the purpose having been found at Sibson as well as Yarwell; eight tables are now working at each place. The discovery of good clay is fortunate, as the stone in the line of the tunnel does not turn out nearly so abundant as had been expected.

Those inhabitants of the Nene Valley living or regularly working near to the river cannot have failed to notice the very considerable increase in river traffic this past month, as work has commenced on the Railway. The daily records kept by the Nene Commissioners, Western Division, and recorded in their Toll Book, of every vessel passing from the Grand Union Canal on to the Nene at Northampton, shows that in February this year five boats carrying in total 85 tons of railway implements, barrows, timbers and other materials for the Railway, passed down the river. In March, however, the Toll Book records 28 boats, 20 of them owned by Mr John Stephenson, contractor, carrying in total about 400 tons of planks and barrows, posts and rails, iron, various timbers, sundries and other railway materials, bound for many destinations along the Nene adjacent to the railway works – White Mills, Houghton, Billing, Cogenhoe, Doddington, Wellingborough, Ditchford, Stanwick, Ringstead, Denford and Thrapston. At Thrapston the materials are either unloaded for use on the works there or continue on to the Nene Commissioners Eastern Division, for deliveries along the line of the Railway between Thrapston and Peterborough. *(The Nene Commissioners' Eastern Division Toll Book for this period does not appear to have survived – JWG).*

The local folk along the valley will only be aware of the railway works near to their own town or village, but in reality we now have a major construction site, with all its attendant problems, just a few yards wide and 48 miles long!

A 48-MILE CONSTRUCTION SITE

By April 1844 the Railway is three months into construction. Work proceeds simultaneously under its separate contracts between Blisworth and Peterborough...

Friday, 5th April, 1844

The *Stamford Mercury* reports that in the course of excavation making at Wansford, numerous Roman remains have been found, and last week the bankers broke into an oven for making pots, which has yielded many barrow loads of broken urns, lachrymatories and vessels of all descriptions. This latter discovery was in a field about 10 yards from the Great North Road near Mrs Boor's house at Sibson. The whole district abounds with such remains.

Thursday, 11th April, 1844

N&P Committee meets. Reference is made to further correspondence received from Mr Wickens, Clerk to Northampton Borough Council and from Mr Barwell, Mayor of Northampton, concerning use of the Truck system of payment for the railway construction workers.

A letter from Lord Lilford, 6th inst, is tabled, requesting that Police Constables be stationed at Thorpe and Titchmarsh. It is ordered that the contractors be requested to make the necessary appointment of Police Constables along the Line, and that Lord Lilford be informed thereof.

Reference is made to Mr Bidder's interview with Earl Fitzwilliam *"...respecting the mode of crossing the carriage road at Aldwalton and had proposed that the Railway should be carried under the road, to which His Lordship had assented".*

Friday, 26th April, 1844

The *Stamford Mercury* reports that Mr Brogden has sent two police officers from Manchester to live in the neighbourhood of Wansford, for keeping in order the immense body of men now working at the Railway there. The officers are endeavouring to get lodgings at Yarwell, but the district is now so full that accommodation is very scarce.

Some hundreds of bankers have accommodated themselves by building huts of earth-sods in the stone-pits; and the wives of a few of them submit to this sort of dwelling. Occasionally there are terrible breezes amongst them: on Tuesday one of the houses, of a larger and better sort than the generality of them, was totally pulled down and scattered abroad, in a quarrel which arose.

Friday, 3rd May, 1844

The *Stamford Mercury* reports that the policemen who were sent from a distance to preserve order at the railway works near Wansford, lodge at Sibson and everything has gone peaceably and pleasantly since their arrival.

The whole neighbourhood is like a hive of bees. On Wednesday a longboat which usually plies on the Grand Junction Canal, arrived at Wansford with a machine from Birmingham for grinding and rolling clay for brickmaking; it was found that the bricks could not be made fast enough without it. Mr Hen. Woods and his men came from Liverpool to fit it up at Sibson, where it is to be worked by steam. Piles for the bridges, etc. are also being driven by steam; and Mr Percival of the Haycock Inn is threshing his corn by a steam engine, which is worked by Mr Tuxford from Boston.

Thursday, 9th May, 1844

N&P Committee meets. A letter is tabled from Mr Wilson, Clerk to the Oundle Magistrates, calling attention to the necessity for the appointment of policemen at Oundle during the progress of the works. Letters from Lord Lilford, Mr Smith and numerous inhabitants of Oundle are also read recommending John Parker for an appointment. It is ordered that the contractor be required to make the necessary appointment of Police Constables at Oundle, and that the recommendation of John Parker be also referred to the contractor.

A letter from Earl Fitzwilliam to the Chairman, 15th ult, is read, expressing his satisfaction at the proposal made of carrying out the works at Aldwalton.

Further payments are approved to the Rhymney Iron Co (for rails), Mr Cameron (for sleepers) and Mr J Stephenson, Contracts Nos. 1 and 2. Land purchased for the Line now totals 528A 3R 0P, for which the Company has paid £102,641 11s 11d. It is ordered that Mr Sanders be instructed to proceed with resale of land not required for the Railway, and to communicate thereon with the Solicitor and Engineer.

Mr Bidder submits the plans and elevation of the proposed station at Northampton. It is resolved that the same be approved and that the usual notice be advertised for tenders to construct the same, such tenders to be delivered on Thursday, 13th June next.

Friday, 10th May, 1844

The *Stamford Mercury* reports that the excavations and embankments for the Railway are progressing very favourably at the works near Wansford. A passage has already been effected for the tunnel, a stratum of sand having been discovered in the Line where it was anticipated stone abounded.

Many persons actuated by curiosity have been allowed already to creep along the subterranean passage from the South Stone Pit, under the Elton Road to the Great North Road at Sibson, though there is certainly some danger of being buried alive in the tunnel, which is not yet arched with any durable material, but is supported by props of wood only, at irregular distances.

Saturday, 11th May, 1844

The *Northampton Mercury* carries an advertisement inviting tenders for the construction of the Northampton station.

The same newspaper also reports on Wellingborough Petty Sessions: Benjamin Bailey, a ganger on the Railway, charged William Birch, Josh. Edmunds and Geo. Lovell with leaving their work and taking away certain tools. The men said they considered they had worked for the tools and all they had received, and complained of the manner in which they had been paid. The Magistrate said the Truck system was a most unjustifiable way of paying the men, and informed the parties that if they agreed to work for so much money per day they could demand it. After further deliberations, reported by the *Mercury*, the men were set at liberty.

Wednesday, 15th May, 1844
N&P Committee meets, and approves the payment of £502 9s 2d to the Rhymney Iron Co for rails.

Friday, 17th May, 1844
The *Stamford Mercury:* "Peterborough – the railway works in the neighbourhood of Woodstone and Orton are now progressing with more earnestness than was shown a few weeks ago, a party of men being employed all night, in addition to those working in the daytime.
"On Wednesday, the workmen in the brickfield turned up some curious carved stones of great antiquity, representing human figures, lions' heads, etc.
"Great improvement has lately been effected on the road between Peterborough and Orton, by the erection of two handsome inns, the 'Gordon Arms' and the 'Cross Keys'."

Saturday, 1st June, 1844
The *Northampton Mercury* reports that Thos. Gunson, a sub-contractor on the Peterborough Railway, appeared upon a summons granted by the Rev Dr Pemberton on the application of William Moore and several other labourers, for non-payment of wages due to them. It appearing from the evidence that these men had not contracted to serve Gunson, but only to do a specific work for him, the Magistrate had no jurisdiction, and consequently was obliged to dismiss the complaint.

Wednesday, 5th June, 1844
N&P Committee meets. Further invoices from the Rhymney Iron Co are tabled and payments totalling £1,567 17s 4d are approved for rails and freightage thereof.

Thursday, 13th June, 1844
N&P Committee meets. Mr Stephenson's estimates for construction of the Northampton station are tabled: in total £12,561 including goods warehouse and engine house, etc. The Tenders submitted are opened and considered in detail; that from Messrs Gwyther and Branson, Birmingham, for £12,130 in total, including warehouse and engine house, is accepted.
Mr Bidder then suggests that the stations at Wellingborough, Irthlingborough and Thrapston should be erected by Mr J Stephenson (contractor for the Blisworth-Oundle section of the Line), and those at Oundle and Sibson by Mr Brogden (contractor for the Oundle-Peterborough section), on condition that they will undertake them at a reduction of 10 per cent from the Board of Works prices for the current year. It is resolved that the suggestion be approved and adopted, the plans first being submitted to this Committee. Letters from Mr J Stephenson and Mr Brogden are then read, signifying their assent to the foregoing arrangements.

Friday, 28th June, 1844
The *Stamford Mercury* carries a report on an event which caused considerable concern to those in the centre of Stamford the previous Friday when 20 barrels of gunpowder were delivered to Mr Grant, ironmonger, in the High Street. These were hastily taken to the works of the Peterboro' railway company at Sibson where they were required for blasting. In Mr Grant's absence Mr Jones, his assistant, appeared before the Magistrates on the Monday to explain the situation and was reminded of the limits placed by Act of Parliament on the keeping of gunpowder.

Saturday, 29th June, 1844
The *Northampton Herald* reports that on Friday last, 21st June, another of those frightful accidents which are so frequently occurring on the line of railway between Peterborough and Northampton, took place near Wansford. It appears that a man

called Ashley was leading away the soil on a tram railway, with a spirited horse, and upon approaching some other wagons the young man, from some unexplained cause, was unable to get out of the way, and was crushed between the projecting ends of the two wagons. He died almost instantly. An inquest was held the following day. Verdict – accidental death.

The same edition of the *Herald* continues... *"Another Railway Accident: On Monday week, 24th June, as some of the workmen on that part of the Northampton and Peterborough line of railway near Oundle were raising a huge block of stone by means of levers, a large piece of about half a ton weight fell upon one of the men, crushing his breast in such a dreadful manner that he only survived about two hours. An inquest was held on the following day when a verdict of accidental death was returned".*

Thursday, 4th July, 1844
The Eastern Counties Railway (ECR) is granted powers to extend from Newport to Brandon, with a branch from Ely to Peterborough to join the L&BR.

Friday, 5th July, 1844
The *Stamford Mercury* reports: *"Almost daily accidents occur at the railway works at Wansford. On Saturday, John Rogers had his collar-bone broken by a mass of stones and earth falling upon him in the tunnel; and on Wednesday at different hours Rd. Briffett (from Somersetshire) and John Anderson (from Peterborough) were carried to their lodgings having met with contusions and fractures from falls through tunnels and scaffolds. Notwithstanding such accidents, the energy with which the works proceed is astonishing".*

Wednesday, 10th July, 1844
N&PR Committee meets. Numerous payments to conbtractors and suppliers are approved, totalling £13,752 10s 0d. Mr Bidder undertakes to confer with the Manager of the ECR respecting the proposed station at Peterborough.

Friday, 12th July, 1844
L&BR Co Way and Works Committee meets. In response to the Directors' Minute 2555 concerning the works for Gayton station (where the N&P Line makes a junction with the main line), the Committee suggests the propriety of postponing the consideration of this subject until after the opening of the Branch Line, when the requirements of the district can be better ascertained.

Friday, 19th July, 1844
The *Stamford Mercury* reports that the number of persons at this time employed on the railway works at Wansford exceeds 1,000. The wages vary from 12s (60p) to 30s (£1.50) per week, the common labourers receiving the former, and the best (or tunnel men) the latter. They are paid every fortnight, at which time a sum amounting to full £1,000 is immediately put into circulation amongst the shopkeepers of that place and the surrounding villages; and the whole proceeds of bread, beer and meat are generally consumed within a few days.

Samuel Clayton, an overlooker of the brickmakers, was apprehended on Monday night and taken into custody to Oundle, for having fraudulently charged his employer (Mr Brogden) 5d (2p) per thousand more than he paid the workmen.

Saturday, 27th July, 1844
The *Northampton Mercury* carries a report on Wellingborough Petty Sessions when a Mr Lovell applied to get the Railway to alter a crossing at Earls Barton. The Magistrates would not grant an order without hearing both sides. (The application was heard again a week later but rejected by the Magistrates.)

Wednesday, 31st July, 1844

N&P Finance Sub-Committee meets. Payments totalling £4,222 6s 1d are approved for the supply of rails and chairs.

During the four-month period April to July this year, some 170 boatloads, around 1800 tons, of railway materials have been recorded in the Nene Commissioners' Toll Book passing from the Grand Junction Canal on to the River Nene at Northampton and proceeding downstream to the many unloading points adjacent to the Railway works. An even greater tonnage, mainly of rails, has passed upstream in this same period, from the Port of Wisbech.

The Nene Valley is witnessing the first signs of the birth of its railway...

"SPARE A COUPLE OF ENGINES?"

It is now August 1844. The Railway is seven months into construction and thanks to a dry spring the work is well advanced. The main concentration of activity at the eastern end of the Line is in the Sibson area. The local press has commended the organisation of the immense body of men working on the Line and reports that at the Contractor's buildings at Sibson a Mechanics' Institute and an evening school are established; also a glee and catch club, and a sick club. But in spite of these cultural and social refinements, theft, assaults, drunkenness, the occasional riot or strike and other social disturbances still abound amongst the workforce on the construction site itself and wherever they roam when not at work.

Wednesday, 7th August, 1844

N&P Committee meets. In addition to the normal items of business dealt with, a letter from Mr Tycho Wing, the Duke of Bedford's Steward, is tabled, offering the Company a house near the site of the proposed Sibson Station. It is ordered that Mr Wing be informed that the Company will not have any occasion for the house referred to as it is the intention to provide the necessary accommodation at the station. A letter is also read from Mr Powys calling attention to the circumstances that the men are employed on the Line on Sundays. It is resolved that the letter be referred to Mr J Stephenson, the contractor for the section of the Line involved.

Saturday, 10th August, 1844

The *Stamford Mercury* reports an inquest held today at the Haycock Inn, Wansford, on the body of Thos. Harden, a labourer on the railway works, who had lost his life in consequence of the accidental overturning of a cart. Verdict accordingly.

Wednesday, 21st August, 1844

N&P Committee meets. A letter is read from Mr R Stephenson requesting that during his absence on the continent, the payments may be made to the contractors on the certificate of Mr Bidder. It is resolved that the request be complied with.

Payment of £425 is approved, to Mr Cameron, for recent deliveries of sleepers.

Saturday, 24th August, 1844

The *Northampton Herald* reports that last Wednesday an inquest was held at Blisworth on a labouring man killed by a fall of heavy timber, while working on a bridge being constructed. Verdict: accident.

Thursday, 5th September, 1844

N&P Committee meets. In addition to the regular items of business a letter is read offering the services of Mr Core and Mr Taverner as Joint Agents for the Railway at the Peterborough station. It is resolved that this offer be accepted and that the necessary arrangements be made accordingly.

A letter from Mr Parker (the Company Solicitor) is then read detailing recent land purchases and compensation payments for the Railway. These include:
Land from Earl Fitzwilliam, Peterborough, for £1195 0s 0d.
Land from Mr J Buckle, Peterborough, for the coalyard, etc., for £1700 0s 0d.
Land from the Misses Smith, Wellingborough, diversion of River Nene, £80 0s 0d.
Compensation to Lord Lilford, Wigsthorpe, £500 0s 0d.

A letter is then read from Mr Sanderson, referring to the serious inconvenience being experienced on the works by the delay in the supply of rails. It is ordered that the matter be referred for the immediate attention of the Rhymney Iron Co and to require that the rails be delivered forthwith. A further letter is read from the Revd M Hartshorne, requesting a station at Cooknoe Mills; referred to Mr Parker. A memorandum is read from Mr Thomas reporting the death of a man on the works by the accidental falling of a log of timber. *(See report of 24th August – JWG)*

Wednesday, 11th September, 1844

N&P Committee meets. In addition to the regular business of approving payments to the three main contractors, a letter is received from Mr Wynn, Rhymney Iron Co in connection with the delay in delivering rails. It is ordered that the Rhymney Iron Co be informed that the Committee require it to be distinctly stated when the rails will be delivered, as the works are delayed for want of them, and further, that the Directors will expect punctuality in the delivery of the remaining quantity which they have contracted for.

Upon receipt of certificates from Mr Bidder, payment to Mr Cameron (for sleepers) and to Mr J Stephenson, contractor, are approved.

Mr Bidder submits plans, sections, etc for the proposed road stations at Wellingborough, Irthlingborough, Thrapston, Oundle and Sibson. His estimate for the Sibson station is as follows:

Booking Office	£2100 0s 0d
Platform opposite	£ 358 0s 0d
Goods Warehouse	£ 878 0s 0d
Rails, turntables, etc	£2270 0s 0d
	£5606 0s 0d

The prices for the other stations are similar, but Thrapston is to have an engine house and a carriage shed, and Oundle a water tank. It is resolved that these prices be approved and adopted.

Tuesday, 24th September, 1844

A lamentable event happened today (reports the *Northampton Herald*), to two of the labourers employed upon the railway works near Wansford, in consequence of the accidental precipitation down one of the shafts. Immediately after the accident the unfortunate men were conveyed to the Haycock Inn, Wansford, where medical assistance was promptly procured, but one of them expired within a quarter of an hour. It was then ascertained that the other sufferer had both his thighs broken and some of his ribs fractured. He survives but lies in a very precarious state.

Wednesday, 25th September, 1844

An inquest is held today at the Haycock Inn, Wansford, on the body of Jas Marsh, blacksmith, aged 40, killed yesterday in the tunnel works, reports the *Stamford Mercury*. The other man, suffering broken ribs, is named as James Arnsby, of Sutton. The newspaper comments that the constantly ocurring accidents make the appointment of Mr Clapham as surgeon at Wansford to the Railway Company, no sinecure.

Also today, at the other end of the Line, an inquest is held on Eli Webb, aged 20, killed at the site of the new Blisworth station, by an earth-fall brought down by vibration of passing trains – reported by the *Northampton Herald*.

Wednesday, 2nd October, 1844

N&P Committee meets. Invoices from the Rhymney Iron Co are received; also certificates from Mr Bidder. The corresponding payments are therefore approved.

Wednesday, 9th October, 1844

N&P Committee meets. Following receipt of certificates from Messrs Bidder and Stephenson, numerous payments are approved. A letter is read from Mr Wynn, Rhymney Iron Co stating that the rails in arrears will be delivered by the end of the month. A letter from Mr Thomas, Blisworth station, dated 25th September, is read, reporting the death of another man *(presumably Eli Webb – JWG)* from the accidental falling of a quantity of earth.

Friday, 11th October, 1844

The *Stamford Mercury* reports that on Friday last, October 4th, an inquest was held at the 'Hare and Hounds', Wood Newton, near Oundle, on William Wadwell of that place, aged 13, who was killed on the preceding Wednesday afternoon, October 2nd, on the Northampton and Peterborough Railway at Warmington, by falling down on the line of rail whilst endeavouring to extricate a horse from the train waggons; before he could get out of the way, they ran over him and killed him on the spot. Verdict: accidental death.

The same edition of the *Mercury* reports that the Bridge Fair (Peterborough) died a natural death on Monday last, 7th October; its successor will be placed in a different situation as the railroad will be upon the late principal thoroughfare. The booths, stalls, etc must be placed nearer to Woodstone.

Thursday, 7th November, 1844

N&P Committee meets. Numerous invoices are tabled and payments totalling £22,019 6s 5d are approved, to the two main contractors, to Mr Cameron for sleepers and to the Rhymney Iron Co for rails. Routine business relating to the conveyancing of land in the parishes of Earls Barton and Barnwell St Andrew is dealt with. A letter is then read from Earl Fitzwilliam, 29th ult, requesting that the bridge for his private road at Alwalton may be completed as early as practicable. It is ordered that a copy of the letter be referred to Mr Stephenson and that his attention be called to Earl Fitzwilliam's request.

Wednesday, 20th November, 1844

N&P Finance Sub-Committee meets. Further invoices and payments are dealt with, for deliveries of rails and sleepers.

Saturday, 23rd November, 1844

The *Northampton Herald* prints a letter, dated November 15th, from a reader referring to Mr R Stephenson's assurance, "*...before he took possession of our valley in the name of his monopolistic employers...*" that drainage of the Nene Valley would not be affected by railway banks, etc.

The letter continues: "*Mr Stephenson... has cut our flood in half, and has driven it far higher towards the uplands than it was ever known to be.*

"*Mr Stephenson has turned loose a torrent upon us, from the neighbourhood of the Paper Mills, on the Bedford Rd... absurdly narrow iron culverts...*

"*It is more, Sir, than any of us bargained for, first to have our fair acres purchased in spite of ourselves, and then to have the adjacent ones rendered at times valueless...*"

(signed) "*Let Well Alone*"

(Following the dry spring, over 13 inches of rain were recorded in the area between July and November this year – JWG).

Tuesday, 26th November, 1844
A further meeting of the N&P Finance Sub-Committee is held. Payments are approved for rails, sleepers and chairs.
Mr Smith brings under the consideration of the Committee his suggestion for laying down a double line of rails between Northampton and Peterborough.

Thursday, 12th December, 1844
N&P Committee meets. Following the regular business of the meeting, a letter is read from Mr Stephenson, 11th inst, stating that the cost of the erection of the stations at Thrapston and Irthlingborough would be much lessened if the L&BR Co could spare a couple of engines for two months to draw the materials, in lieu of the horses at present employed for that purpose. It is resolved that the application be referred to the Locomotive Committee, with the recommendation of this Committee that it be complied with if possible.
A memorandum from Mr Creed is read, of the importance of the early opening of the Line to Wansford. The Chairman reports that he had been informed by Mr Bidder that the Line would be ready for opening throughout by 1st April next.

Friday, 13th December, 1844
The *Stamford Mercury* reports that a fatal accident occurred on Tuesday last to a labourer named John Rose, employed at one of the shafts of the Wansford railway works. He was engaged with others raising a large block of stone to the surface by a gin, when the harness of one of the horses broke; the other horse was thrown off the ring and part of the machinery struck the unfortunate man across the thighs, nearly severing one of them from his body. He was immediately conveyed to the Haycock Inn and died in about two hours. Rose was a native of Melksham, Wiltshire, and has left a widow and four children. Veredict at the coroner's inquest: accidental death.

Friday, 20th December, 1844
The *Stamford Mercury* predicts today that the Railway will be completed by Lady Day and will be open to the public for travelling by the 1st of May next.

Saturday, 21st December, 1844
The *Northampton Mercury* reports that an absurd rumour has become prevalent in the town that a train was about to convey passengers to London at 1s 6d ($7^{1}/_{2}$p) each. The *Mercury* continues: *"We are authorised to state that it is totally without foundation"*.

These last five months have probably seen the peak of activity in the constrction of the Railway; considerable lengths of track have now been laid and the gaps are closing daily. Between August and the end of November around 200 boatloads of railway materials have made their way off the Grand Junction Canal and down-stream to the construction site. Amongst them, on 29th November, was a solitary cargo registered as 'cement and chimney pots' bound for Thrapston or beyond. Rails have continued to come the other way, from the Port of Wisbech.

Now it is late December: only eight boats have arrived this month, for the Canal and all the Nene Valley are frozen over. There is an air of optimism as the Railway begins to take shape, but the deaths and injuries on the works these last few months have cast a dark shadow as we wait for the thaw.

ENTER MR COOKE; LOCOMOTIVE ARRIVES

January 1845 and we are now eleven months into construction. Much of the track is now in place and there is local speculation that the line will be opened to the public by the 1st of May this year...

Friday, 3rd January, 1845
N&P Finance Sub-Committee meets. Payments totalling £3127 11s 7d are approved, to the Rhymney Iron Co for rails, and for the freightage thereof from the ports to locations along the construction site.

Thursday, 9th January, 1845
N&P Committee meets. Numerous items of business are tabled and discussed, including further payments for rails, sleepers, etc and a claim for £10 0s 0d for five days' demurrage of the ship *Thomas*, having delivered a cargo of rails.

A letter is read from Mr Parker (the Railway Company's solicitor) enclosing a resolution from the Northampton and Bedford Road Committee complaining that the road was recently flooded in consequence of the works on the line, and calling for the erection of a screen fence at St Peter's Bridge (Northampton). It is ordered that the letter be referred to Mr Stephenson for his report thereon.

Friday, 24th January, 1845
The *Stamford Mercury* prints a report concerning the proposed route of the Midland Railway line from Syston through the district of Stamford, which it is feared will present competition with the line from Blisworth to Peterborough.

The same newspaper also reports: "...*the surveyors and others engaged in the works of the Blisworth and Peterboro' Railway by Wansford assert that the line will certainly be completed by Lady Day next; and we have reason for believing that the Post Office authorities contemplate some changes of the mail routes at that time... Peterboro' will be supplied by railway; and the Lincoln and Stamford Mail will probably receive at Wansford the letter bags for the north and part of the east of Lincolnshire. It is calculated that the mail will reach Wansford about one o'clock in the morning and Peterboro' a few minutes afterwards*".

Wednesday, 19th February, 1845
N&P Finance Sub-Committee meets. Payment of £8144 11s 9d to J Stephenson, contractor, in respect of Contract No 2 is approved. Referring to a decision of the Directors of the Railway Company, it is ordered that a meeting of the London members of the N&P Committee be summoned for Wednesday next and that Mr Cooke be requested to attend on the subject of the Electric Telegraph.

On this same day, reports in the *Stamford Mercury*, the Northampton newspapers and the *Railway Times*, the first engine on the Blisworth and Peterborough railway was placed upon the rails at the Thrapston station. The engine, in passing through Northampton, was drawn by 16 horses.

Wednesday, 26th February, 1845
N&P Committee meets. The Directors' Minute 2781 is read, authorising the laying down of the Electric Telegraph on the Line. It is resolved that Messrs Cooke and Wheatstone be requested to furnish this Committee with their tender for laying down the Telegraph on the N&P Branch Line, with two wires so adapted as to admit the addition of two more wires if at any time found necessary.

Mr Bidder attended the meeting and read the following resolution of the Northern & Eastern Railway Board: "*That the Plans prepared by Mr Stephenson for the Peterborough Station be submitted by him to the London & Birmingham Board for their approval, and when approved, that the Directors of this Company will proceed with the construction thereof, and will fix with that Board the rental to be paid by the London & Birmingham Committee for the use of the same Station*". It is resolved that Mr Stephenson be authorised to approve the Plans on behalf of this Company and that he be requested to urge the immediate erection of the Station.

Friday, 28th February, 1845

The *Stamford Mercury* reports that although the 1st of May is the day named for the opening of the line, it seems to be doubtful whether the works at Sibson will be sufficiently advanced by that time to enable the Company to open it this early. Railway contractors, the *Mercury* continues, are generally bound to complete the works at periods mentioned in the contracts, the non-fulfilment of which subjects them to the payment of very serious sums to the Company; in the case of this railway the contracts, it is said, have been broken, caused by the Company not being enabled to complete the purchases for land before the time arrived for the contractors to begin work.

Preparations are being made, the newspaper continues, for the immediate erection of the station in the Horse Fairground at Peterboro', a large quantity of bricks having been carted there for that purpose and the outer walls of the orchard belonging to the Crown public house having been thrown down.

Wednesday, 5th March, 1845

N&P Finance Sub-Committee meets. A letter is read from Mr Cooke, 25th ult, making a tender for laying down the Electric Telegraph on the Northampton and Peterborough Line and stating that he had commenced his preparations for the execution of the work. It is resolved that the consideration of Mr Cooke's tender be adjourned until the general meeting of the Committee on the 13th inst. and that Mr Long be instructed to inform Mr Cooke that as the Committee has not decided on the extent to which they will adopt his suggestions, he had better not proceed any further in his operations for the present.

Friday, 7th March, 1845

The *Stamford Mercury* reports that the expected opening of the Line on the 1st of May next is already affecting the demand for coal in the district. It is expected that good coals will be brought by the railway from the Swannington pits (near Leicester) to Blisworth, and thence to Peterborough, at the price of 14s a ton delivered at the latter place; and about 16s delivered at Stamford from Wansford.

Thursday, 13th March, 1845

N&P Committee meets. In addition to the normal business of the Committee, a deputation from Wisbech is received concerning the conveyance of the Mails over the Line. It is arranged that they should consult the Post Office authorities and communicate thereon to the Committee.

Tenders are then read from Mr Cooke, 25th ult. and 12 inst, for laying down the Electric Telegraph. The Committee, having had a conference with Mr Cooke, resolve that Mr Cooke lay down the Electric Telegraph between Blisworth and Peterborough, with three wires on the following terms:: Mr Cooke to receive payment for the prime cost of the materials employed – the bills being submitted for Mr Stephenson's examination – and Mr Cooke to receive in addition £40 0s 0d per mile for the use of his patent and £10 0s 0d per mile for his time in superintending the erection of the telegraph, the use of his workshops and any other contingency, the Company having the benefit of any improvements.

A letter is read from Mr Howes, Northampton, 10th inst, complaining of the danger attendant upon the passage of the ballast engines across the Turnpike Road on the level, in the absence of gates and Police Constables. It is ordered that the letter be referred to Mr Stephenson with instructions to order the erection of the necessary gates as early as possible.

It is also ordered that Mr Long be instructed to inform Messrs. Pickford & Co that this Company is willing to erect separate goods sheds for them at the Northampton and Peterborough stations on their undertaking to take a lease of such sheds for 21 years at a rent equal to seven per cent per annum on the outlay.

Friday, 28th March, 1845

The *Stamford Mercury* prints a letter from a correspondent on the Blisworth Railway, dated Wednesday, 26th March:

"I went to see the railroad at Sibson (Wansford) today. They have got fixed four large gates and four small ones on the Turnpike Road opposite the line there. They have also got the roof on the station house and on the warehouse and have fixed many pens for sheep and beasts.

"I was told that some of the inspectors belonging to the Birmingham Company are to come next week with a carriage and the steam engine which are now lying at Thrapston

"There are still upwards of 300 hands employed within a quarter of a mile of the tunnel east and west, getting as much done as they can by the time the inspectors come. The 'navvies' and others, as they now gradually withdraw from the works, leave bills unpaid in all the villages where they could obtain credit with tradespeople or those who let lodgings; the losses sustained are in many areas very severe. And not only does the district suffer in a pecuniary way from the visits of these freebooters, but fellows have taken many women from the neighbourhood, and in some instances the wives of decent men and the mothers of families, who have been induced to rob their husbands and abscond".

Saturday, 29th March, 1845

A fatal accident befell an 8-year-old boy today at Northampton, reports the *Northampton Mercury*. He was crushed in the gates at the London Road level-crossing. Thos Ludgate, the gatekeeper, was unable to hold back the gates after the passing of a ballast train because of the crowds pushing.

With the earthworks virtually completed and most of the track in place, it is hardly surprising to find the local press and the general public speculating on the opening of the Railway and the expected benefits once the trains start running.

The last three months have seen nigh on 200 boatloads of materials pass from Northampton to the many points along the new railway mostly in boats owned by John Stephenson. Deliveries of rails from Wisbech, by far the greatest tonnage involved in the work, are now virtually complete.

At the Peterborough end there is building work to complete, track to lay across the Bridge-Fair meadow while the Electric Telegraph has not yet reached the city.

As the opening day approaches it is now a race against time...

THE END OF THE BEGINNING

By April 1845 the Railway, after nearly fourteen months of construction, is expected to be open to the public by the middle of next month. Train times are already being speculated on in the local press and it is said that a locomotive and carriages lie ready at Thrapston. But there is still work to be done...

Thursday, 10th April, 1845

N&P Committee meets. A letter from Messrs Pickford & Co, 15th ult, is read expressing their willingness to lease the sheds on the terms stated, conditionally that the sheds are erected on their plan and that the cost is approved by their surveyor. It is resolved that Messrs Pickford & Co be instructed to request their surveyor to put himself in communication with the Company's engineers. A letter is also read from Mr Cooke, 20th ult, re the electric telegraph between London, Birmingham, Liverpool, Manchester and Holyhead.

Referring to Mr Cooke's contract for the N&P line, it is resolved that he be required to state his terms for continuing the telegraph from Blisworth to Wolverton.

Mr Bidder, having stated that the line cannot be opened throughout to Peterborough earlier than the 1st June next, and the Committee being exceedingly anxious that it should be opened as far as Stamford, by Wansford, on the 15th May which Mr Bidder states can be done, it is resolved that Mr Bidder be requested to prepare the working tables for this partial opening.

Also, it is ordered that Mr Parker (the Railway Company's solicitor) be instructed to give the necessary notice to the Board of Trade.

In addition to other business, further payments are authorised:

Mr Cooke on account of Electric Telegraph £2500 0s 0d.

Messrs Covington & Co for Lighterage of rails £148 1s 10d.

Mr R Stephenson, Engineering account £1250 0s 0d.

Friday, 11th April, 1845

Today the *Stamford Mercury* asserts that there is no longer any doubt that the line of the railway from Blisworth to Peterborough will be opened with some ceremonies on the 1st May. It is said that an engine and carriages will run along the whole line on the 16th inst.

Friday, 25th April, 1845

The *Stamford Mercury* reports that it is now found that the Line cannot be opened so soon as the 1st of May; it is expected that the ceremony will take place about the middle of the month... The tunnel at Sibson is now completed and is open to daily visits of hundreds of persons, who are much gratified with the stupendous work.

Saturday, 26th April, 1845

The *Northampton Mercury* gives a detailed account of a fatal accident involving a locomotive and ballast waggons near to Duston Bridge. A train being pushed by a locomotive collided with and was derailed by 'cross-rails' (used by horse-drawn waggons) having been left in position.

Wednesday, 30th April, 1845

N&P Committee (Finance Sub-Committee) meets. In addition to normal items of business, payments are approved to:

The Revd Edward Barton Lye, Rector of Raunds, £10 0s 0d and the Revd John Sargeant, Rector of Stanwick, £8 10s 0d – being annual rent payments for land taken by the Railway.

Payments totalling £3610 15s 4d are also approved, for the supply and treatment of sleepers.

Friday, 2nd May, 1845

The *Stamford Mercury* acclaims that tomorrow, Saturday, at about 10 or 11 o'clock in the forenoon, the first train with the Directors of the Railway from Northampton, it is expected, will reach the Sibson station; and it will then be settled at what time the public opening shall take place; the 15th inst is named as the probable day.

The beautiful station house at Sibson is of the Elizabethan order... and was built by Mr Thompson of Barnack; this bears the palm, though several of the other station houses on the line to Blisworth are beautiful buildings. The opening on (or about) the 15th will only be to Sibson; it will take yet some few weeks to complete the line to Peterboro'. About 50 men employed in raising gravel at 14/- a week struck for wages on Tuesday last, which in some area retards the work.

Saturday, 3rd May, 1845

Today (reported by the *Stamford Mercury*) and according to appointment, a special train started from Euston Square, containing several of the Directors of the London and Birmingham Company, with Mr Bidder, the acting engineer, on an experimental trip upon the Northampton and Peterboro' line. The party had ordered that dinner be prepared at the Haycock Inn at Wansford, on their return from Peterboro', but changed their minds and returned as far as Thrapston 'ere they dined. All things, it is understood, satisfied them on their view; and the middle of the present month was appointed for a formal opening of the Line to the public as far as Sibson from Blisworth, a distance of 41 miles.

In the interim arrangements are being made for a change of the mail routes, as it is expected that the Lincoln and Hull mail will, very soon after the opening of this railway, be dispatched by it to Sibson and thence will be forwarded at one o'clock in the morning by coach to Stamford, Bourn, Sleaford, Lincoln and northwards...

When the line is completed to Peterboro' from Sibson... we understand there will be four up trains to London daily, and the same number of trains downwards to Peterboro'. The fares, we understand, will be moderate – 12s (60p) from Peterboro' to London in a first class train, or 21s for going and returning, to and from London. The Act provides that one train per day shall carry passengers at 1d per mile. At Peterboro' there is to be a joint station for all the railway lines converging at the point as soon as they are completed.

The train which conveyed the Directors today consisted of a locomotive engine, two first-class carriages, a luggage carriage and a tender, and arrived at Peterboro' at about 12 o'clock. The parties remained in the city about two hours and then started back, after having attracted the attention of a large number of persons.

An electric telegraph is in course of erection, and is, we understand, in a state of much forwardness, particularly at the Northampton end of the line. Some of the pillars containing the non-conducting and conducting compositions are being placed upon the line at Woodstone. One of the two extraordinary large gates crossing the line of railroad and the turnpike near The Crown at Fletton, has recently been fixed and has excited attraction.

Tuesday, 6th May, 1845

L&BR Way and Works Committee meets. It is reported that the Committee has let the formation of the road to the new Blisworth station, and also the widening of the bridge over the canal, to Mr Richard Dunkley at £1635 0s 0d.

Thursday, 8th May, 1845

N&P Committee meets. Numerous general items of business are dealt with. An extract from a letter from Mr Beasley is then read, complaining of having been stopped on the Line by one of the contractor's men and very roughly treated.

Further letters are read from the Trustees of the Northampton and Cold Brayfield Turnpike Road, complaining of the want of culverts to carry off the water in times of flood and requesting that a screen fence may be erected at the point where the railway and Turnpike Road run close to, and parallel, to each other. It is ordered that the letters be referred to the Company's engineer for immediate attention. It is also ordered that a further payment of £1500 0s 0d be made to Mr Cooke on account of the Electric Telegraph.

It is resolved that in the opinion of the Committee the opening of the line throughout to Peterborough should take place on Saturday the 31st of the present month and notice to that effect should be given to the Engineers, the Solicitor and Messrs Home and Chaplin.

Tuesday, 13th May, 1845

The *Northampton Mercury* reports that at the request of the Mayor of Northampton, the Northampton to Blisworth section of the Line is opened to the public today, for Whitsun. The first train left Northampton at 7.00 am for London, the passengers being allowed to return free by 6.00 pm Wednesday or Thursday. The train carried between 200 and 300 people from Northampton – 400 by the time Euston was reached. A train now leaves Northampton every morning at 7.00 am and returns from Euston at 6.00 pm.

Fares: 1st Class 14/-; 2nd Class 10/6; 3rd Class 5/-.

Wednesday, 28th May, 1845

This afternoon (later reported by the *Stamford Mercury*) a train from London arrived at Sibson, to remain for the holiday *(and formal opening of the line – JWG)* on Monday next. Notice of its approach was given by the electric telegraph an hour before its arrival.

Friday, 30th May, 1845

Today's *Stamford Mercury* states that on Monday next the Peterborough and Northampton Railway will be formally opened and the citizens intend to have a holiday on the occasion. Bands of musicians are engaged; a public dinner will take place at the Angel Inn and coaches will come in from Lincoln, Sleaford, Louth, Boston, Spalding, Lynn, Wisbech, etc to go by the several trains from the Peterboro' station. The permanent metals are being laid across the embankment in the Bridge-Fair meadow, in preparation for the opening of the railway on Monday.

A petition, we understand, is in course of signature by the various shop assistants and others in Peterboro' to their employers praying that business may be suspended from 12 o'clock on Monday next, for the rest of the day.

Saturday, 31st May, 1845

Today (quoted from a letter later printed by the *Stamford Mercury*) a special train, conveying a party of Directors and their friends, left the London terminus at half past nine o'clock for the purpose of opening and inspecting this additional line of traffic, which is stated to be the longest branch yet made from any trunk line. It is entered at a short distance from the Blisworth station on the London and Birmingham line, about 63 miles from the metropolis, and after traversing a level tract of pastureland, reaches in four miles and three quarters a neat station on the southern side of the populous town of Northampton. Here the party received an accession by the arrival of the Mayor and other corporate authorities and the train, now increased to 15 first-class carriages, proceeded on its route.

By a rather circuitous course, following the meanderings of the beautiful River Nene through a country picturesque and highly cultivated, studded with pretty villages and churches of architectural pretensions, the unfinished stations at Castle Ashby, Wellingboro', Ditchford, Higham Ferrers and Ringstead were passed and we paused at Thrapston. Thence, passing Thorpe and Barnwell stations, after a call at Oundle, the train, still keeping the windings of the valley, and passing Fotheringhay, the scene where poor Mary of Scotland ended her chequered and blighted reign, we reached the Sibson or Wansford station, after traversing the only tunnel on the line – about half a mile in length. Here a communication is opened with Stamford, lying six miles and a half north of the station. Between Stamford Road and Peterboro' the views of Castor, Milton Park (the seat of Earl Fitzwilliam) and the imposing towers of the adjacent cathedral are of great beauty.

The time occupied in traversing the whole of this branch line, a distance of $47\frac{1}{2}$ miles, was about $2\frac{1}{2}$ hours, including stoppages occupying above 50 minutes.

After a brief stay, which the visitors generally devoted to a hasty glance at the exterior and interior of the beautiful cathedral, a retrograde movement was effected at a slower pace, and the train, after stopping as before, reached Wolverton shortly after six o'clock, where a collation was prepared for the company and they reached Euston Square about half past ten, much pleased with the day's excursion.

This new line, comprising only a single line of rails between Northampton and Peterboro', has been completed in 15 months at a cost of £10,000 per mile, considerably under the estimate.

Sunday, 1st June, 1845

The Line is inspected by General Pasley, the Inspector-General of Railways. Reporting on the event the *Stamford Mercury* comments on the imposing nature of the train in which General Pasley and a large company arrived at the Wansford station on Sunday evening about six o'clock from London; this Sunday train consisted of three engines and 27 carriages and the speed with which it approached Wansford from Oundle is supposed to have been scarcely less than a mile a minute; anything more superb than the sight which it presented can hardly be imagined.

The sound of the train on the railway (resembling a hard rushing of water) was distinctly heard at the Sibson station for full 20 minutes before the train arrived.

General Pasley was expected there at two o'clock but did not arrive till six, an electrical message being sent from the Sibson station to Northampton at half past five, to enquire the cause of the delay; an answer was returned *in four minutes* that the General had been waiting for as many carriages as he could collect in his train (an experimental one), and would be at Sibson at six o'clock; and so he was to a minute. He proceeded to Peterboro' and the same night returned to London.

In consequence of the arrangements not being yet complete, continues the *Stamford Mercury*, it is reported that the Company is not at present prepared to convey heavy goods.

Monday, 2nd June, 1845

Today is appointed for the opening of the line to the public – reports the *Stamford Mercury* the following Friday – an event which will be long-remembered by the many thousands of persons who witnessed the proceedings of the day.

The first up-train left Peterboro' station (which is a capacious place on the east side of the London Road a few hundred yards from the bridge) at 7 o'clock in the morning, with six carriages, and another train followed at half past ten with a goodly number of passengers; and this latter met the first down-train from London at the Wansford station, where the latter arrived shortly before 12 (at least one hour after its appointed time). The passengers from London, Northampton, Wellingboro', Higham Ferrers, Thrapston, Oundle, etc. having filled the first train to Peterboro', the greatest disappointment was experienced at Sibson station where at least 200 persons were waiting to proceed by it to Peterboro'; a few did succeed in getting upon the roofs of the carriages, but the more respectable company were left behind and had their ticket-money returned.

On this train's approaching Peterboro', a most interesting scene presented itself to the voyagers, many thousand persons having congregated to witness the arrival of the first public railway train into that city; and although the population was under 7000 at the taking of the last census, it is believed there must have been from 10,000 to 12,000 persons present – every town and village for some miles around having assisted to make this extraordinary assemblage.

The majority of the company occupied the meadow where the celebrated bridge-fair is held, but the bridge and the road thence to the turnpike were also densely crowded with anxious spectators, as also was every window from which a view of the train could be obtained. It was stopped on the west side of the road for the purpose of receiving the passengers' tickets, which occupied about a quarter of an hour, and after this the road was crossed on the level and the train approached the station, in Fletton parish, amidst the plaudits of the throng, the ringing of the church bells and bands of music.

The moving mass then crossed the River Nene and entered the city, at which time at least half the shops were closed and those who were ready to wait upon their patrons seemed to have little or nothing to do. The inns generally were very crowded and from the presence of so many strangers the landlords must have experienced a good harvest.

The interval which took place between the arrival of the first train from London, and that of the second, which was advertised to arrive at a quarter to 3 o'clock, was occupied in taking refreshment and in visiting the cathedral and the shows; the latter consisted of Ewing's wax-work exhibition, a theatre and several other attractions of less importance which were stationed in the market-place.

Vast numbers of persons again proceeded towards the station, but the second train from London did not arrive till after the time of the departure of the 4 o'clock train from Peterboro' was announced in the timetable. Parties desirous of returning home by the latter train procured tickets and took possession of the carriages, which were soon crowded to excess inside and out, and many at this time had no chance of a place. Some tried to ascend the roofs of the carriages, but were as speedily compelled to desist. The probability of being left behind caused much confusion and unpleasantness and one affray which took place proved very alarming; a man who had come for some distance along the Line in the morning was determined if possible to return by this train and made several unsuccessful attempts to gain the roof of a carriage, which was already very crowded – indeed, so much so, that there was not then room for all who occupied this part to sit down – a position rendered necessary to pass under the bridges with safety. Ultimately he succeeded in getting up and this, exasperating a gentleman (from Weldon) who had been extremely anxious to keep him down, the latter struck the intruder with a thick stick. Both parties possessing similar weapons, a determined fight took place between them, to the imminent peril not only of themselves, but of course those who were so unfortunate as to be placed near them.

At about half past four o'clock the second London train, which had then been due an hour and three quarters, arrived, also densely crowded with passengers, and the scene that took place was of a very amusing character. Probably three-fourths of the persons by this train were desirous of returning by that which they saw already filled, and many of their countenances evinced extreme mortification on their finding that they should be compelled to remain. They soon scampered out of the carriages and rushed for their tickets and when they were told that they would be sent back by the carriages that brought them, their anxiety was appeased, but many of the more timid still thought there would not be room for all of them. The whole of the carriages then located at this station were soon filled and at seven minutes to five o'clock the train started on its journey.

Between Peterboro' and Sibson there are several bridges to pass under and as there was not sitting room for all who occupied the roofs of the carriages, the greatest difficulty was experienced by the men having charge of the train in getting many of the passengers to stoop sufficiently to prevent accidents and there was much reason to fear that something serious would occur.

However, in a quarter of an hour after leaving Peterboro' the train arrived safely at Sibson station, where a large portion of the company got down, and at several of the succeeding stations many others left, but on approaching nearer to Northampton the passengers again increased in number.

It is very gratifying to observe that everything passed off pleasantly, with the exception of what took place at the station at Peterboro', as alluded to above, and we did not hear of a single accident occurring during the day. It was a subject of regret with those left behind at Sibson that the Railway Company did not provide more carriages, as it was reasonable to suppose that a very large number would avail themselves of the first opportunity of taking a trip by railway.

The *Stamford Mercury* continues – There was a public dinner at Mr Taverner's, The Angel Inn, Peterboro' in the afternoon, which was attended by about 50 persons, including coach-proprietors from Boston, Spalding, Deeping, Stamford, etc. The chair was taken by Dr Scrimshire and T Miller, Esq acted as vice. After dinner many toasts were proposed and speeches made, in the course of which the importance of the undertaking they had met to celebrate was forcibly dwelt upon, and occasionally the superiority of travelling by rail to that of coach was spoken of in such terms as excited the displeasure of some of the "old gravel men", as the stage proprietors are now called, but the thing most complained of by the latter was the allusion to accidents which had occurred to their conveyances for many years past, whilst not one of the mishaps on the rail was alluded to. Dr Scrimshire having left the chair, Mr Whitwell was voted to it, but by this time it was discovered that all the coach proprietors, with one exception, had left and gone to another room. On the cause of the disappearance being asked, the remaining proprietor alleged that the illiberal remarks made in reference to coach accidents had induced them to retire. It, however, being the wish of the company that the meeting should pass off pleasantly, the absentees were waited upon and they agreed to return to the dining room. Much discussion followed, which afforded amusement to the silent observers of the scene, but eventually the best feeling prevailed.

At most of the bridges and roads along the line large numbers of persons had congregated and received the trains with hearty cheers. The cattle in many instances, unaccustomed at present to the noise of the engine, were seen running about in great terror; near Milton three horses broke from a waggon and ran with the broken harness for about two miles over hedges and ditches.

An incident which caused some amusement to the passengers by the afternoon train from Peterboro' was witnessed near the above place; some boys about ten years of age were bathing in the Nene and on seeing the train approach, the novelty induced them to leave the water and run to the side of the line, where they clung to some rails to see the train pass. Being in a state of nudity, they attracted the amused attention of the passengers and the age of the boys allowed even the females to smile at the circumstances.

The electric telegraph was called into requisition, the *Mercury* continues, and although the cause was not of an important character, it showed how useful this invention is likely to prove. Mr Chapman, the coachman belonging to the Lincoln Tally-Ho, allowed his greatcoat and whip to be sent on by the train, but discovering the accident shortly after the train left, he went to the gentleman who works the telegraph and mentioned to him his loss. Before the arrival of the train at Oundle, the circumstance was known at the station there and on its arrival the property was secured and returned to its owner. The wire alone for this telegraph has, it is said, cost the Railway Company £17,000.

It is almost 2 years and 7 months since the Directors of the London and Birmingham Railway Company resolved that it *"...would conduce to the public accommodation and the particular interests of this Company"* to construct a branch railway connecting Peterborough, the intermediate towns and places and the adjoining districts with the London and Birmingham Line near Gayton.

Construction work began just over 15 months ago and has cost at least 11 lives, with many more injuries and narrow escapes.

The folk of the Nene Valley have experienced, for the first time ever, the onslaught of industrial "progress", and life along the Valley will never be the same again.

Now the Railway is open to the public – but this is only the beginning...

PETERBOROUGH VIADUCT.

A train from Northampton is about to pass under a train from London on the GNR's viaduct. The artist (A Ashley) has sited the Nene Valley line closer to the river than it was and placed the cathedral on a hill.

Peterborough Museum Society

Chapter Three
YARWELL

The Northampton and Peterborough Railway's presence at Yarwell is more generally associated with the junction at that place which was not installed until 35 years after the opening of the Nene Valley line. Yarwell Junction was situated at a point 37 miles from Northampton Castle Station, $43\frac{1}{4}$ miles from Rugby, one mile west of Wansford Station and $7\frac{5}{8}$ miles from Peterborough (East) Station. The site of the junction was about a hundred yards south of the River Nene in the Parish of Sibson-cum-Stibbington where the railway lay on an embankment which raised the line above the flood plain of the river. The village of Yarwell could be seen on rising ground some distance away to the north.

However, Yarwell was an important site during the building of the line as the River Nene was used to bring construction materials in to that area. Contemporary newspaper reports reveal that brickmaking machinery was brought there by the river for use in connection with the work on Wansford tunnel which was brick lined throughout. This was a large operation with raw materials, clay and fuel coal being landed from the river and finished bricks being moved to the tunnel, it making sense to locate plant as near as possible to the tunnel yet close to the river to reduce transhipment. The Ordnance Survey 25 in map for 1889 shows a small inlet off the river near the tunnel, this being shown in greater detail on an LM&SR 1934 plan of Yarwell Junction which was prepared for proposed quarry sidings. This inlet appears to have been a water-filled hollow extended by some 90 ft with an indication of a dip in the land for some 100 yds before rising ground. Although no source contemporary with the building of the tunnel mentions the existence of an inlet off the river and there is no reference to it in the deeds, it is hard to see any other purpose for the feature marked on the plan other than something directly connected with the tunnel's construction. Clearly the railway would use any means possible to reduce to a minimum the distance heavy and bulky materials had to be moved overland. The deeds do however reveal the existence of a quarry between the proposed tunnel and the river at about its Yarwell portal. It is thus possible that instead of digging the full inlet the railway simply connected existing quarry workings with the river to provide an economical means of moving construction materials as close as possible to the tunnel workings. The inlet was abandoned and silted up after work on the tunnel had been completed and no signs of the inlet survive today due to quarry operations from the 1930s to the 1970s. However, stone was taken out by river barge from Yarwell until recent times.

On 12th June, 1845, ten days after the railway opened to the public, a Conveyance was made between the Rev William Wing, Rector of the Parish of Stibbington, and the L&BR Company which recorded the purchase of just under five acres of land from what became the site of Yarwell Junction east to the Elton Road, which ran over the tunnel, for £215 or about £43 per acre. This Conveyance gave " ...me and my Successors Rectors of the Parish of Stibbington otherwise Stepington *aforesaid free right and liberty at all times hereafter..."* to have two pipes or culverts which were provided at specified places *"...under the said Branch Railway..."* to be maintained in good repair by the Company. Another provision of the Conveyance related to a roadway which crossed the line at one of the culverts in that the Conveyance was extended to include *"Tenants Agents Servants Laborers and Workmen"* of the Rector or his successors and give them *"...free liberty at all times to cross and recross the said Branch Railway either on foot or with carts carriages cattle or horses or otherwise at the point or place hereinbefore described... and for that purpose the Roadway across the said Railway with the approaches thereunto which have been made by the said Company shall for ever be maintained in repair by the said Company at the expense of such Company..."*. Any crossing of the railway was required to be made *"...so as not to interfere with the said Company in the free and uninterrupted use and enjoyment of the said Railway nor to damage or injure the Works thereof"*.

Seventeen months after the opening of the Nene Valley line an accident occurred approximately at the site of the future junction. According to the *Stamford Mercury* for 20th November, 1846, *"Saturday last, within 500 yards of the west end of the railway tunnel at Wansford, an empty luggage train overtook and ran upon another and broke some trucks belonging to the loaded train, beside knocking a hole in the engine of the empty one. The accident was owing to their moving in the twilight at 6 o'clock in the morning. The men all jumped off the trains and were very little hurt. The empty train was going for a load of cattle which were waiting at Peterborough to be taken to London"*. Signalling arrangements in 1846 were very primitive with trains being controlled by the Time Interval System where the aim was to keep successive trains apart by a given time period.

As mentioned in the Introduction, the Nene Valley line provided an indirect route between Peterborough and the Midlands, the reversal at Blisworth Junction and its longer journey, both in distance and time, making it less favourable than the Midland Railway's more direct route. As traffic increased over the years between the Eastern Counties and the Midlands the L&NWR, in the early 1870s, finally decided to build an 11 mile cut-off line between its Northampton and Peterborough line and its Rugby and Stamford line. The cut-off line between Yarwell and Seaton was authorised on 21st July, 1873. It was a good example of nineteenth century railway politics in that agreement on the building of the line was interconnected with events in other places; the link between the building of the cut-off line and the dispute between the S&ER over its Wansford branch junction with the L&NWR is related in the chapter on Wansford.

After authorisation, construction of the double track line went ahead. In 1878 a temporary signal-box was installed to the south at what was to become Yarwell Junction which allowed contractor's trains access to the new line. A catch point was installed west of the junction to protect the main line. A permanent junction signal-box was opened in 1879 on the north side being located 1 mile 37 yards from Wansford and 1276 yards from Nassington Station on the new line. This was a standard L&NWR type with a brick base and wood top, and contained a 20-lever frame. The Seaton-Yarwell line opened to goods traffic on 21st July, 1879 with passenger services commencing on 1st November.

Signalling through Yarwell Junction changed very little over the years. The original track diagram in the box was dated 13th February, 1879 and only appears to have required minor corrections in May 1947. The year 1934 saw some realignment work being undertaken on the junction probably to increase the speed through it. In the mid-1930s there were various proposals for stone quarry sidings between the line and the river west of the tunnel but none of these were proceeded with.

According to a LM&SR Working Timetable, the speed restriction through the junction was 40 mph Up and Down on the Northampton line, but 20 mph Up and Down on the Seaton line.

In the 1960s came line closures with through passenger and freight services being withdrawn on both the Northampton and Rugby lines though a freight service was retained to Oundle and iron ore traffic continued from Nassington Quarries. The lines were downgraded with the inevitable reductions in track work. From Sunday 1st January, 1967 Yarwell Junction signal-box was closed, to be demolished soon afterwards; the Yarwell Junction shunt spur (the former Up line to Oundle) was cut and slued into the Oundle single line (the former Down line from Oundle), the former Up line to Oundle being lifted. All point work was removed and the junction transferred to Wansford. The Yarwell-Wansford former Up line now became the Oundle single line and the former Down line the King's Cliffe single line. Two train staffs were provided from Wansford, one for each line. The direction of working was now Down from Peterborough East to Oundle/King's Cliffe and Up to Peterborough East.

The traffic to Nassington continued until the quarries closed in December 1970. They were the last completely steam-worked iron ore quarry system in Britain. On 1st January, 1971, Hunslet 0-6-0ST *Jacks Green*, which had spent its working life in these quarries, with the headboard 'Nassington Flyer' worked under its own power from Nassington to Peterborough to join the Peterborough Railway Society's engines at the British Sugar Corporation sidings in Woodston. From 26th September, 1971, when Wansford signal-box was disconnected, the points at Wansford were permanently set for Oundle and a single train staff was introduced between Peterborough and Oundle. The Oundle School Special, which had run to/from Kings Cross at the start and end of each school term and required a reversal at both Peterborough North and Peterborough East, ceased in 1972 when BR announced its intention to close the line.

Early in 1975 Thomas Ward commenced lifting the Oundle line west of the centre of Wansford tunnel. So far as the trackbed was concerned, when the L&NWR purchased the land for its Seaton line, there was a clause in the agreement that if the line was ever taken up the original owner or his heirs could exercise the right to re-purchase at the original selling price. This right was exercised by the Proby estate in 1978.

Chapter Four

WANSFORD

WANSFORD STATION IN ITS EARLY YEARS (1845-1869)

Wansford Station was located 600 yards to the east of Wansford Tunnel at a point where the Northampton and Peterborough Railway crossed the Great North Road by a level crossing and then bridged the River Nene. The station was 6½ miles east of Peterborough and 37 miles from Northampton (Bridge Street). It was built in the parish of Stibbington-cum-Sibson which was one mile from the village of Wansford, the combined population of both parishes in 1851 being only 971. While the railway was under construction and for a number of years following its opening the station was sometimes referred to as Sibson and an early timetable gives the station's name as Wansford (Sibson); here Wansford will be used.

Regarding land at Wansford, two deeds covered the area between the eastern part of the tunnel and the river crossing. The first deed was an Agreement between the Duke of Bedford, Rev William Wing and the L&BR dated 25th March, 1844, and was only concerned with the tunnel. The second, dated 12th June of that year, was a Conveyance which dealt with that part of the tunnel east of Elton Road, the cutting, the station site, and the land between the Great North Road and the river, all belonging to the Duke of Bedford. Both deeds gave details about the construction of this section of line. However not all the figures in the deeds agreed as to the cost of the land and the acreage purchased. In the sale Wing received £130 and Bedford £370 though according to the Conveyance Bedford received £851 for just under eight acres from Elton Road to the river (about £106 per acre).

The sale was complicated by Bedford having no documentary proof of title to his land and relied on a declaration of ownership by one John Wilson, aged 21, who had lived all his life in Wansford and was acquainted with his Lordship's estate. The fields concerned were known as Peaks Grave field, Woodgate Way field and Potters field. The future station was built in the latter, the name referring to discoveries of Roman pottery with more being found during construction.

The station building was designed by John William Livock in a fashion which reflected, in a rural setting, the grand style of the L&BR termini. It was built of stone in a Jacobean style by Thompson of Barnack at an estimated cost of £5606. Wansford was the main station between Oundle and Peterborough due to its location beside the Great North Road and the fact that, in the 1840s, Wansford was the nearest rail point to Stamford. Stamford was seven miles away and the connecting coach with that town took one hour. In 1845 Wansford was described as being an important station having extensive sheds, cattle and sheep pens and yards, the station building having an elegant Booking Office and Waiting Room said to partake of the same elegance and convenience as the other stations on the line.

One person who recalled the building and opening of the railway at Wansford was Thomas Hazeldine, a postman at Wansford Post Office whose delivery round took him to the surrounding villages. One place he delivered letters to was the navvy colony at the 'Hills and Hollows', outside Elton village, where woden huts were built in a former stone quarry whose steep quarry face formed the rear of each hut. He also remembered the excitement of the locals when the first train arrived as they had only confused ideas as to what a railway engine was really like.

With the opening of the Nene Valley line Wansford welcomed its first passengers, the original fare from Peterborough to Wansford being First Class 1/- (5p), Second Class 9d (4p) and Parliamentary 7d (3p). The journey took, on average, 15 minutes although staff inexperience during the first few months of operation caused frequent delays. River traffic had been important to Wansford before the arrival of the railway especially as after the Grand Junction Canal had been built London could be reached up river via Northampton. Much of this traffic was lost once the railway opened.

Alexander Campbell is known to have been the Clerk in Charge of the station in 1847. The Station Master some time before 1851 was Thomas Dixon who was succeeded in the 1860s by George Day. In 1851 Dixon was assisted by a staff of four porters – Edward Clothier, Thomas Dawson, Jeremiah Preston and Samuel Taylor. Dawson's father, also called Thomas, was at that time listed in the Census as a coal dealer most probably at the station though previously he had been a tenant of the Duke of Bedford. By 1867 the station staff had increased to about seven including three Railway Policemen – Joseph Blain, Henry Newland and William Sewell. The presence of Railway Policemen, an early description for signalmen, does not necessarily mean that Wansford's first signal-box was opened some time in the previous decade as in this early period it was common practice to operate signals and points individually from the line-side.

In 1867 Wansford became a junction. As early as August 1845 plans existed for a branch line to Stamford and in 1846 an Act authorising the construction of such a branch was actually passed while in the following year a deviation via Sutton, Southorpe and Pilsgate was being discussed. These plans came to nothing. It was not until 8th August, 1867 that the Wansford branch of the Stamford and Essendine Railway was opened with its single track line joining the Nene Valley line, by now part of the L&NWR, 80 yards east of Wansford Station. However, in 1869 a dispute arose over the amount the S&ER had to pay in rent for the use of the L&NWR station and as no agreement was reached the junction was removed.

The importance of Wansford was reflected in the complexity of the station layout. In 1878 the L&NWR applied to Parliament for additional powers to improve the station's facilities and the plan associated with this application shows the layout prior to that year. The original road approach to the station was on the Down (north) side. The main building consisted of a ground floor Waiting Room and Booking Hall with the Station Master's accommodation upstairs. Beside the level crossing, squeezed between eight railway cottages and the Down line, was a very small signal-box which was reputed to be so narrow that signalmen were issued with leather waistcoats to protect their backs when pulling levers!

As was common on the Nene Valley line, the two platforms were not directly opposite each other with the Up (Northampton) platform being further to the west. This platform only had one face and on it was a waiting shed; the bay platform on the south side was not built until later in the century which disproves the suggestion that from its earliest years trains from Stamford terminated in the bay platform. Clearly such trains must have used the main line platforms and been shunted into sidings if anything on the main line was due. In any case the turn-out into the

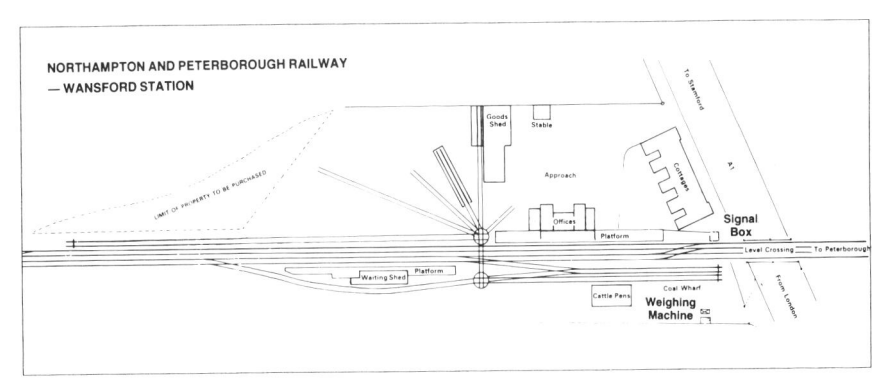

Wansford Station in 1878. Diagram drawn from the original plan in Huntingdon Record Office by Don Crick

bay for a train approaching from the east was wrong way on. On this south side there were however two sidings, which terminated not far from the Great North Road. Beyond were cattle pens, a coal wharf and a weighing machine. At this time there was no footbridge to link the two platforms.

Probably the most notable features on the plan are two wagon turnplates and the connecting wagon road which crossed the main lines at right angles between the two platforms. This dangerous practice, common in the 1850s and 1860s and later outlawed, did enable goods facilities to be provided on one side of the line only requiring a horse to transfer wagons over the tracks so saving on costly point work and shunting. Off the Down wagon turnplate ran no less than six lines, one of which went into a large goods shed which was near to the stables which perhaps housed both carriers' horses and a shunting horse. It should be noted that at this time there was no direct connection between the Down line and the goods yard.

WANSFORD STATION IN LATE VICTORIAN AND EDWARDIAN YEARS (1869-1914)

As stated above, Wansford became a junction in 1867 with the opening of the branch line from Stamford. It is possible that the returns from passenger and freight traffic on the S&ER branch were a disappointment from the start which led to the dispute with the L&NWR in 1869. In November of that year the L&NWR refused to grant a rent reduction and consequently on 1st January, 1870 the junction was severed, the track lifted and sold. The S&ER now erected a hut beside a short length of platform on their side of the former junction. As this halt was also called Sibson the name used by the L&NWR for their station from then on was Wansford. The village of Wansford now had the dubious distinction of being served by three stations all of which were some distance from the village, the third being the S&ER's Wansford Road which was situated beside the main Peterborough to Wansford road. To link the new halt to the L&NWR station, the S&ER constructed a raised causeway leading to a footbridge 100 yards north of the L&NWR's bridge over the river. A more logical route would have been to follow the stone causeway under the L&NWR flood arches and to use the latter's footpath across the Nene. However, the route under the flood arches, as the name suggests, would not have been passable all the year round.

The front of Wansford Station c1900   Photo: Originally published by F Howard & Co
— NVR Archives

Wansford Station from the Up (Northampton) island platform c1910   Photo: NVR Archives

Negotiations to re-commence through running started in 1871, but it was not until 1873 that agreement was reached whereby the L&NWR, for an annual rent of £150, would undertake to make and maintain the junction. The existing signal-box and signals of the S&ER company were to be handed over to the L&NWR who would appoint a signalman to control the junction. At least four trains daily in each direction, except Sundays, were to be provided on the branch while in addition the L&NWR were to stop a similar number of trains at Wansford. The L&NWR were also given running powers along the Wansford branch but it is doubtful if these powers were ever exercised. Despite this agreement, and for some unknown reason, services did not resume over the junction at that time.

In July 1875 an ideal opportunity to remake the junction arose when, after two days of heavy rain, the S&ER footbridge, path and fencing were washed away. Far from remaking the junction the relatively expensive option of rebuilding the footbridge was chosen. The new structure consisted of a brick main arch which spanned the river with smaller arches on either side and was of such a permanent nature that it survived until being demolished in February 1975. John Rhodes in his book *Great Northern Branch Lines to Stamford* appears to have found the reason for the rebuilding which stems from an Agreement in 1872 between the S&ER and the GNR and required the Master of the Milton Hunt to have free passage over the bridge. The bridge was therefore also for horses and hence why it was sometimes referred to as a horse-bridge. Mr Rhodes' researches further suggest that the rebuilt bridge was privately owned and was constructed by the Rev William Hopkinson of Sutton Grange. Clearly the footpath on the L&NWR river bridge could not have accommodated horses. Within three years the junction had been restored and through running resumed on 1st March, 1878. The reason for this turnabout appears to be that the L&NWR were forced to reinstate the junction to avoid the opposition of the Marquis of Exeter and others to their proposal for a Seaton to Yarwell line.

There is some uncertainty as to whether, when through running resumed, S&ER trains terminated at the main line platforms as they did before the junction was lifted or whether they used the new bay platform on the south side of the island platform. If the bay had not been built by the time through running resumed, then it must have been built soon afterwards. The opening of the Yarwell Junction to Seaton link in 1879 and the subsequent opening of the GNR's Fletton Loop in 1883 brought an increase in traffic through Wansford. With such an increase the blocking of the main line by a terminating train would no longer have been an acceptable practise.

In 1877 Stephen Reay, Secretary of the L&NWR, notified the Board of Trade that *"...the junction with the Stamford line at Wansford, which has for some time been disused, has been reinstated"*. There followed an inspection by Col William Yolland who was very critical of the arrangements he found. The junction was controlled by a small signal-box on the south side of the L&NWR lines but the points at the Stamford end of the short section of double S&ER track were found to be 198 yards distant, too far for safe working from this box. Col Yolland called for certain improvements which probably explains why through running into the L&NWR station by Stamford trains did not resume until March 1878. He then turned his attention to Wansford Station and was again critical. As to the very small signal-box located between the end of the Down platform and the crossing he found that it had levers which were in the open while its interlocking was incomplete as was that for the junction signal-box. The practise of shunting wagons over the turnplates was also condemned by Col Yolland.

In view of the various criticisms, the L&NWR made their application to Parliament, in 1878, for additional powers to improve the station's facilities, as previously mentioned, which included additional land to the north-west of the goods yard.

Acquiring the additional land did not involve purchase as is shown by a deed dated 12th December, 1878 between Hastings Duke of Bedford and the L&NWR. By this deed one-quarter of an acre of land required by the railway for its goods yard approach was exchanged for two plots of land beside the river at Sibson linches. The two plots together were of about the same area with one to north and the other to south of the railway. Sufficient space was still left beside the railway for development. As a result both platforms were extended, a proper connection was made with the goods yard enabling the wagon crossing to be removed, and the signal-box arrangements were changed.

In September 1879, the Board of Trade returned to inspect the new arrangements, by which time there were three signal-boxes. A new signal-box (No 1) with 24 levers had been provided to control the western end of the station and this box was beyond the island platform on the Up side. The signal-box (No 2) by the level crossing still existed it having 34 levers and controlled the level crossing area. The signal-box (No 3) controlling the junction had 15 levers, was probably a new structure, and Ordnance Survey maps for 1885 and 1899 show it to be positioned 40 yards to the west of the previous junction box. It was not until the 28th April, 1907 that signalling was concentrated in one signal-box, situated on the Down side between the level crossing and the river, whose 60 lever frame controlled the network of tracks around the station. The GNR contribution towards the cost of this box was £75.

Station Staff in 1910: standing – Bertie Tilley (S.M.), Fred Middleton (Clerk), Fred Waite and Gerald Longfoot (Porters), F C Lee (Signal and Linesman); seated – William Coles and Charles Kidsley (Signalmen).
Photo: NVR Archives

The station staff at Wansford in 1871 numbered seven, including Laurence Jinks as Station Master who was succeeded by a Mr Padmoor in 1876. Robert Marshall held that position from about 1877 until about 1903 and in 1881 had a staff of nine including his son, Robert, who was a clerk. The Census of 1891 showed that Marshall lived in the Station House with his wife, Isabella, and his daughter, Mary. Mr Marshall was succeeded by Bertie Ernest Tilley, who remained there until the First World War, and was assisted by a staff of eight. When Fred Waite joined the station staff as a junior porter, before 1914, his first wage was seven shillings. He was still working on the line in the Second World War by which time he had become the senior passenger guard based at Peterborough East.

Contrary to the popular impression that Wansford was quite a rural station, the three decades prior to the First World War were very busy. In the 1880s there were seven trains (weekdays only) each way on the Wansford branch with additional trains on Fridays. Of the trains on the Peterborough-Northampton line, six trains in each direction (weekdays only) were booked to stop at Wansford. The opening of the Yarwell-Seaton line added a further five trains each way which also called at Wansford while the opening of the Fletton Loop brought a further three trains each way (weekdays only) which called there. During the 1880s a total of 42 passenger trains, every weekday, stopped at Wansford and to this number had to be added goods, special passenger, departmental and other trains. By 1910 a further two trains were calling at Wansford each weekday. While Wansford was certainly not Clapham Junction it was far from being a sleepy country station. As to goods facilities, a wharf plan of 1907 shows that Siddons were then the coal merchants who were responsible for two structures in the yard plus the stables.

WANSFORD STATION IN THE FIRST WORLD WAR AND INTER-WAR YEARS (1914-1939)

The outbreak of war in 1914 brought increased military traffic through Wansford. While military traffic increased Wansford saw a curtailment of unnecessary passenger services. Fred Waite recalled that at the outbreak there was a great fear of German spies and sabotage as a result of which a Special Constable, armed with a revolver, was sent to each signal-box. Once while messing about with the gun it went off! Until the 1960s the bullet holes could still be seen in the woodwork of Wansford signal-box.

If the layout of Wansford Station at about the First World War is compared with that prior to 1878 a number of changes are apparent. In addition to the two main platforms, linked by a footbridge, Wansford now has a bay platform for the S&ER branch trains. The old wagon line at right angles to the main line which gave access to the goods yard has been replaced by a four road goods yard with a goods warehouse, cattle pens, a horse and carriage landing stage and a coal wharf with office accommodation for George Siddons and Sons, Coal Merchants. From a 1914 plan no hand crane is apparent, but in 1929 a crane of 1 ton 15 cwt capacity existed. The goods' facilities were therefore typical of a country station able to deal with traffic in coal, farm produce and livestock. On the Up side beyond the bay, there was a loop which enabled S&ER locos to run round their train without using the main line. From this a short headshunt ran which terminated close to the Great North Road. Beside this was a permanent way stores hut, a platelayer's cabin and a linesman's office. Locomotives were never stationed at Wansford and when required they came from the L&NWR loco depot at Woodstone. As to the station staff, Bertie Ernest Tilley who had been Station Master from the turn of the century, was still there in the First World War. He was succeeded in that position by Henry Lines in about 1920 and later by Frederick W Alton who was Station Master from about 1924 until the mid-1930s.

The 1920s and 1930s brought a number of changes. Some pre-war services reappeared including, in July 1921, the through Harwich boat train which had been withdrawn some time during the war. In October 1921 there were six passenger trains each weekday in each direction that stopped at Wansford on the Northampton line and five each way on the Rugby line. Four trains each way ran on the S&ER's Wansford branch to Stamford. There were also a number of proposals to change some of the facilities at the station. In 1926 there was a plan to raise the low Up platform to standard height and in 1933 there was a proposal to build a sleeper dock 5 ft above rail level to allow lorries to tip sand and gravel. Three years later, in 1936, Central Tar Distillers Ltd proposed to build a tar distillery to the west of the Great North Road and the LM&SR produced a plan showing siding accommodation at Wansford to rail connect the distillery to the existing sidings on the north side of the station. In the following year a proposal was made to slew the cattle dock to give passenger stock clearance. None of these proposals was ever implemented.

In view of the station's location beside the Great North Road the growth in road competition was particularly obvious during the inter-war years and Wansford experienced falling passenger and goods traffic. With more traffic using the Great North Road the level crossing became a serious bottle-neck with staff dreading foggy weather when vehicles frequently crashed through the gates.

The Wansford branch was the first victim of road competition. During the 1926 Coal Strike, two trains were discontinued, never to be reinstated. In 1929 the closure of the line was being discussed and on 21st March, 1929 a report presented to the L&NER Traffic Committee stated that the branch *"...has been worked at a loss of about £3,000 a year. Consideration has accordingly been given to abandoning the branch altogether as there is no prospect of any development on or adjacent to the line and the loss is likely to increase rather than diminish in view of road competition"*. The annual rent for the GNR (L&NER) use of Wansford Station and ten chains of track amounted to £427 10s 0d (£427.50). Passenger services ceased on 1st July, 1929 and the track was removed before 1931. Upon closure the L&NER were to pay the LM&SR £250 each year in compensation although a lump sum of £5,000 was eventually agreed. Closure of the branch caused some hardships especially that of Wansford Road Station to housewives living in Upton who used to shop in Peterborough. After closure they had to walk to and from either Wansford Station, via the river footbridge, or Castor Station as there was no bus service at that time.

By 1938 thirty-two passenger trains each weekday were calling at Wansford, eight each way on the Northampton line and seven Up and nine Down on the Rugby line, some terminating at Seaton. On summer Saturdays a Northampton-Yarmouth service called at Wansford, Castor and Orton Waterville while on such Saturdays between 1936 and 1939, there was a Birmingham to Yarmouth train via the Nene Valley line.

Passenger traffic on the Nene Valley line at that time was rarely heavy with some of the most crowded trains being those which conveyed school children from country stations, such as Wansford, to and from schools in Oundle and Peterborough. Mr S N Edis, between 1937 and 1939, regularly travelled from Wansford to Peterborough where he was a pupil at Fletton Grammar School. His friend was the Station Master's son and after school they would return to Wansford where Edis would sometimes play with his friend's model railway on the station Waiting Room floor, to the amusement of passengers waiting for their trains.

The problem with the growth of road traffic along the Great North Road, especially in foggy weather with vehicles crashing through the level crossing gates, has already been mentioned. One accident occurred in 1932 when, just after the signalman had closed the crossing gates, an early articulated tanker from a Scottish distillery jack-knifed with the tanker ending up on its side across the tracks. Fortunately an oncoming train was stopped in time. The signalman found that the tanker had split its side and its precious cargo of raw spirit was running out over the road, across the adjacent allotments and into the river. It was not long before thirsty railwaymen could be seen running out of the cottages with every pot and pan they could lay their hands on! Although in the short term they were able to celebrate their good fortune, in the longer term nothing would grow for years on the allotments as the spirit had contaminated the soil.

There were at least three accidents in 1938 and 1939, the worst being in early June 1939. In this incident a lorry driven by Herbert Ashworth of Holdsworth was on its way to London with a load of blanket material from Dewsbury. At 1.14 am, as Mr Ashworth approached the crossing gates which were closed to road traffic as a train was approaching, the brakes on his lorry failed. He caused his lorry to swerve so that it went through the wooden fence to the right of the crossing rather than through the gates. The lorry continued over the two running lines, hit a stone wall and overturned on to the Up line. Seconds later the 12.40 am express goods from Peterborough East to Birmingham ploughed into the wreckage flinging the lorry, which had caught fire just before impact, on to the Down line near the station buildings. Fortunately Mr Ashworth had managed to jump clear and was uninjured. Mr C F Seaton, the then Wansford Station Master, and the occupants of the eight railway cottages soon arrived to give assistance.

The locomotive, which had remained on its track, was soon able to set back to clear the crossing. By the time the fire brigade had extinguished the fire the heat had cracked some of the station windows, burnt sleepers and distorted rails. A breakdown gang from Peterborough managed to clear the wreckage so that by 5.30 am the express goods could proceed with caution. The fire-damaged sections of track were replaced soon afterwards and the line re-opened. During the night the 2.40 am from Rugby to Peterborough and several goods trains were diverted via Seaton. Apparently some of the blanket material was salvaged for, as an old railwayman has told, when war broke out a few months later there was no shortage of blackout material in the neighbourhood!

WANSFORD STATION IN THE SECOND WORLD WAR AND UP TO NATIONALISATION (1939-1948)

On 1st September, 1939, two days before war was declared, the Government took over control of the railways and, as in the First World War, operating controls were introduced to make the most effective use of the railways. Non-essential passenger services were curtailed with priority being given to the movement of the armed forces, war materials and munitions. It is not known how many trains passed through Wansford in an average 24 hour period, but an observer on the platform would have witnessed a continual stream of traffic. The Second World War for Wansford was the busiest time the station was ever to experience.

Special prisoner of war trains were run, there being an extensive Italian Prisoner of War camp near Sibson Airfield which occupied the fields to the south of Yarwell Junction between the tunnel cutting and the junction itself. Men and materials came by train to the various air bases in the area, the nearest being King's Cliffe Airfield where the USAF 20th Fighter Group was based after December 1943.

Despite the military camps in the area, Wansford was never bombed and escaped the war unscathed. However, when in January 1945 a flying bomb exploded near Castor Station, as related in the chapter on that station, Driver Newell on a Down passenger train was delayed at Wansford until the line was reported safe. The names of the wartime Station Masters are not known.

With peace, the decline of the railway resumed despite which improvements to the level crossing were carried out in 1946. In the severe winter of 1947 a locomotive became stuck in the cutting near the tunnel and Driver Newell remembers helping to dig the engine out. Unfortunately as soon as it was free, but before it could be moved, a snow plough train from Rugby to Peterborough passed at speed on the adjacent line and shot the snow back again. The gang's comments are best not repeated and one line remained closed until the following day!

On 1st January, 1948, the railways were nationalised with the Nene Valley line becoming part of British Railways, London Midland Region.

WANSFORD STATION FROM NATIONALISATION TO LINE CLOSURE (1948-1972)

In the post-nationalisation years with the massive increase in road traffic the station saw further decline. As the station was some distance from Wansford village, and little freight traffic was generated locally, its days were numbered.

It is understood that Mr Coleman was the Station Master during the late 1940s and early 1950s but in December 1954 he was succeeded by Albert Spicer. Shortly after Mr Spicer arrived he also became responsible for Castor and Orton Waterville stations while in 1956 his responsibilities were extended to cover Nassington, King's Cliffe as well as Wakerley and Barrowden. At Wansford he was assisted by three signalmen and one porter, John Chambers. Mr Spicer remained at Wansford until 1961 being its last Station Master after which Ray Pollard, the Oundle Station Master, became responsible for those stations formerly under Wansford's control.

Mr Spicer recalls that during the 1950s passengers from Wansford Station fell because of its distance from the village there being, on average, about twelve regular commuters and about as many casual travellers each day. There was also some parcels traffic which varied according to the season being particularly busy at Christmas. Freight traffic was not extensive with about six wagons of coal arriving each week while Bibbys, the agricultural merchants who stored animal feed in the goods shed, required several loads of feed weekly. Outward goods included cattle and sheep for market, and wool in season. Seasonal farm produce included seed potatoes and grain for which thousands of sacks were hired out and received back. As Wansford had a side loading dock the occasional car or military vehicle could be accommodated. Most traffic was local, with a few items going long distances. Wansford being a typical small country station was able to deal with whatever traffic came its way.

There was a plan in February 1953 to close the station, remove the footbridge, the canopy on the Down platform and the buildings on the Up platform, and cut back the platform edges. On 1st July, 1957 the station did close to passenger traffic though the Northampton line and Rugby line services continued until the mid-1960s. Wansford's closure caused some hardship due to the infrequent and slow bus service in the area. The footbridge and canopy were removed soon after closure to passengers while the Down brick platform, which was only eighteen inches high, was shortened some time between closure and 1960. The structures on the south side, except a brick permanent way hut, were demolished by 1965. The points by the level crossing which had given access to the bay platform had already been removed in September 1948.

Kings Cross Division outing at Wansford in 1967. Sir John Betjeman stands between *(l)* **Colin Morris and** *(r)* **Edwin Howell, senior members of the Division. The Divisional Manager, Dick Hardy, is on the right and next to him W O Bentley.** Photo: R H N Hardy

In the 1950s the problem of the level crossing over the busy Great North Road became acute. Perhaps the last accident to occur before the opening of the A1 by-pass, which bridged the railway, in 1959 was on 9th July of that year. On this occasion, as a south bound lorry loaded with long steel tubes approached the crossing, the gates began to close. The lorry driver, James Young, braked only to be hit in the rear by a second vehicle driven by Thomas Ashton. The impact forced the steel tubes forward crushing the cab and trapping Mr Young and his mate Percy Reed. A permanent way gang, which was working on the line near the station, along with two ladies from the Station Cottages, Mrs J Fielding and Mrs F Langford, believed to be railwaymen's wives, rushed to give assistance. By the time the vehicle could be moved a tailback of traffic over a mile long had formed.

Despite money having been spent in 1963 to make Wansford's goods shed vermin proof, goods facilities at the station were withdrawn on 13th July, 1964. Following the withdrawal of passenger services came the inevitable track reductions and in July 1967 the station was put up for sale as an *"...away from it all..."* country cottage near the Nene. The goods yard was advertised as being capable of development into a road haulage depot with sidings to provide a *"possible direct rail link with Birmingham"*! Either in the late 1960s but at least before 1971 the sidings into the goods yard were removed with the exception of the siding into the dock. The goods shed was not demolished and subsequently formed part of an enlarged warehouse; the former weighbridge also survives.

On 1st January, 1967, with the closure of Yarwell Junction signal-box and its junction being severed following the loss of through traffic, stop boards were erected between the A1 road bridge and Wansford Tunnel. The former Down line became the Oundle line and the Up line became the Nassington line, access to the Oundle line being by the cross-over just east of the A1 bridge. Both the Oundle and Nassington lines west of Wansford were worked on the one engine in steam principle. From 26th February, 1967 the Down line from just east of Wansford River Bridge to just west of the level crossing was lifted with the Down line through the station becoming a spur. The Down line from Peterborough East to Wansford was then used as an engineer's siding and for training staff in track maintenance machine use while the corresponding Up line was worked on the staff and ticket system. Wansford signal-box finally closed in September 1971 and its rodding was disconnected; it subsequently became a chicken coop.

The year 1967 saw the station building and yard being sold to a road haulage contractor with the station being used at times as offices though it suffered long periods out of use. The cottages were also sold at about the same time. In December 1973, just over a year after BR had closed the line, the station buildings and the adjacent cottages were listed under Grade II as buildings of special architectural or historic interest, while in 1990 the signal-box was similarly listed.

WANSFORD IN THE 1950s – The Memories of Albert and Mrs Spicer

As mentioned above, Albert Spicer was the Station Master at Wansford from December 1954 to 1961 and he and his wife have spoken of their memories of Wansford. Before taking up his appointment, Mr Spicer came to Wansford Station for his interview in the autumn of 1954 travelling by bus from Peterborough. Not knowing of the closed S&ER branch he confused the former Wansford Road Station for his destination and then found that he had a 1¼ mile walk via Wansford village to the BR station.

He recalled that two of Wansford's staff lived at Nassington these being Jack Sumpter, a relief signalman, and Jack Woodward, a relief porter at Castor as well as Wansford. Other railway employees lived in the station cottages between the station approach and the level crossing. Some of the signalmen had gardens on either side of the line which ran down to the river. Among the railway staff there was a strong sense of community and one Christmas Mrs Spicer remembers drinking tea and rum into the early hours with the signalman and had to be helped down the steep signal-box steps! She also mentioned a fish and chip van which used to call at Wansford station yard once a week; a portion then only costing 9d (4p).

As will be seen from chapter five, after Mrs Spicer had passed an examination, she was appointed crossing keeper at Castor Station. During her test, the inspector asked her what class certain locomotives belonged to, her reply being that she knew little about locomotives but supposed they were either 1st or 2nd class! The inspector's reply is not recorded.

On foggy nights there were frequent accidents at the level crossing as traffic along the Great North Road was very heavy and the approach from the north was curved and slightly down hill. The Spicers kept a filled picnic basket and a lamp by their bedside. If there was an incident Mrs Spicer, who was a qualified nurse, would attend to the injured while Mr Spicer would unhinge the damaged crossing gate. Mr Spicer remembered that driving animals along the busy Great North Road was very dangerous though some animals came to the station via the old S&ER horse-bridge as did pedestrians to and from Sutton. The opening of the Wansford by-pass in 1959 made life much easier.

Mr Spicer spent much of his time with administration, particularly with the hire and return of grain sacks, and had to deliver wages to staff who lived at Castor and Orton Waterville stations. One duty of a Station Master at that time, which he did not get pleasure from, was to attend closure meetings to present BR's case. Station Masters used to be on call one week in two and Mr Spicer worked alternate weeks with his opposite number at King's Cliffe being expected to turn out in all weathers if circumstances demanded it. One winter's night when he was the duty Station Master for King's Cliffe, a light engine from Seaton Junction failed to appear and he had to walk way past King's Cliffe before finding the engine stuck in drifts in a deep cutting. On another occasion, close to Christmas, the Wansford signalman stopped an unfitted goods which had arrived divided and this time Mr Spicer had to walk almost to Wakerley and Barrowden before finding the rear portion. There was also a tragic event about 1956 when a teacher committed suicide at Mill Lane bridge in Castor by walking in front of a goods train. On arrival at Wansford the driver reported the incident and Mr Spicer rode on the light engine back to the bridge where he found the teacher's clothes folded neatly on the side of the cutting. Mr Spicer remembered that members of the Royal Family frequently travelled to Barnwell by train which mean extra work. Before the passage of a Royal Train along the line, as Station Master he had to walk his patch and staff had to be placed at all gates, crossings, bridges and culverts; quite a major undertaking.

The rule book was always important to railwaymen and Mr Spicer soon found he had a problem on coming to Wansford as the lines from Peterborough to Northampton and Rugby were penetrating lines between BR's Eastern and London Midland Regions. Wansford was operationally under Rugby (LMR) Control but commercial aspects were dealt by Peterborough (ER) offices and the different areas had developed their own traditions. At some point the operation of the line was transferred to the ER which caused some confusion as on the LMR Up was to Euston via Northampton or Rugby while on the ER Up was to King's Cross via Peterborough. It took some time before the new arrangements were finally understood by all.

As Station Master, Mr Spicer lived 'above the shop' in the station house. Mrs Spicer remembered the stone walls were very thick and the building was difficult to heat. In fact condensation was a major problem and it was not unusual to find water running down the stairs. This problem was never solved, although Mr Spicer had work done on the elaborate chimney stacks which reduced water penetration. Upstairs the Spicers had three large bedrooms, the middle room being the largest with an additional small room at the rear, away from the platform side. Two staircases, one at each end of the building, led up to a long corridor, a wooden partition running its full length. Mr Spicer thought that this internal division indicated that the upstairs rooms had been used as offices. A small room at the west end contained old station furniture when the Spicers first arrived at Wansford. On the ground floor, from west to east, a side door led into the porters' room with one of the staircases that led upstairs. Outside this door was a small garden. Next was the disused lamp room, after which there was the Waiting Room with a ladies WC at the rear. Then came an oak panelled Booking Hall followed by the Booking Office. The Station Master's private lounge and then the dining room/kitchen were next while at the east end, and to the rear, was the scullery. Outside at the east end were the Station Master's private yard, WC and coal store with the garden beyond. Passengers gained access to the station building by a central door on the north side which led into the Booking

Hall while another door on that side led into the Station Master's rooms. There were a number of doors on the platform (south) side which led into various parts of the building.

Some time after moving in the Spicers discovered that the building had a ghostly occupant, being said to be haunted by an old lady. On several occasions the Spicers heard movement in the corridor at night and could smell a strong scent of lavender while their children would not go upstairs alone when they were young. As support for this the Spicers pointed out that when friends stayed the night, some would quite independently report a presence the following morning.

WANSFORD RIVER BRIDGE

Wansford River Bridge, known to the railway civil engineers as Bridge No 56, was one of thirteen such bridges which took the Nene Valley line over the river. It was built at a cost of £1045 being sited just north of a row of several cottages, long since demolished, which stood between the Great North Road and the river. There must have been a public ferry in operation here at some time as one cottage was known as Ferry House. A footpath ran from the east side of the river to Sutton village and this might have been the reason why the railway provided a footbridge on the downstream side of their bridge. According to the *Stamford Mercury* work started on the bridge and its approach embankment in January 1844. The contractor was Mr Brogden of Manchester and Messrs Wright and Russell of London were sub-contractors. By April of that year a steam piler was in operation and eleven months later the adjacent level crossing gates were installed.

According to C R Clinker, the original bridge was of wood with one track only being laid for the opening of the line in 1845. He believed that the original rails were laid on stone sleepers these being replaced when the line was doubled in 1846. Some of the stone blocks are thought to have been used in the construction of the footpath under the bridge on the Castor side of the river most of which can be seen to this day.

It is possible to trace the history of the bridge through various old plans. A L&NWR plan stamped 'Engineers Office Stafford, 24th May 1862' dealt with the bridge's proposed reconstruction. Stone piers were to be strengthened to support cast iron girders while a footbridge was shown on the south side. With traffic increasing in volume and becoming heavier, the bridge periodically required upgrading. A L&NWR plan stamped 'Engineers Office Northampton, 24th July 1880' was concerned with stays for the parapet girders while a further plan stamped 'Crewe, 6th Febrtuary 1894' contemplated renewal. In the interests of economy the possible use of second-hand cast-iron girders was investigated, suitable examples being at Walsall and Northampton. No action appears to have been taken for a plan dated 14th September, 1897 proposed strengthening the bridge by addition additional girders between those existing on both spans on the south side and on the Wansford side span on the north side. A note indicates that this work was completed by 27th July, 1899. A further plan stamped 'Engineers Office Permanent Way Department, Crewe, 19th October 1909' showed details of steelwork for the reconstruction of the cast iron spans, the contractor being EG & J Keay of Birmingham. This is the most recent plan of the bridge that has been located. No plans from LM&SR or BR days are known to have survived.

Wansford River Bridge taken from upstream c1890.   **Photo:** *Peterborough Museum Society*

The photograph of Wansford River Bridge was taken from upstream with a small steamboat about to pass underneath it. The footbridge steps on the Castor side of the river can be seen through the left arch while the row of cottages, which were subsequently demolished, are visible just above the bridge parapet on the right of the photograph.

In 1990 Wansford River Bridge was listed under Grade II as a building of special architectural or historic interest.

WANSFORD TUNNEL

The only tunnel on the Nene Valley line was located at Wansford. Work on it started on 25th January, 1844 at South stonepit with a Mr Jones from Sheffield being the contractor. A week later work began on sinking the first of three shafts, the other two being started about the middle of March. It had been expected that 136,000 cubic yards of earth would have to be removed at each end before stone was reached, the hope being that this stone could be used for embankments on the line. The stone was not as abundant as had been expected with sand and blue clay, mixed with small sea shells, being found instead though had there been more stone it would not have benefited the railway as had been hoped. The tunnel was brick lined to a thickness of six half bricks, i.e. 2 ft 3 in. Bricks for the lining were made not only at Yarwell but also on the Sibson (Wansford) side of the tunnel where suitable clay had also been found. Three months from the start of tunnelling a passage had been made throughout and visitors were allowed to creep along this passage though there must have been some danger as it had not been arched by then but was only supported at irregular intervals by props of wood.

The land for the tunnel was covered by the two deeds mentioned at the beginning of this chapter, the purchase price for the land being £500. The Agreement is the more interesting of the deeds as it reveals that the tunnel required the purchase of some 2½ acres of land of which half an acre west of the Elton Road was glebe-land being part of the benefice of the Rev William Wing, Rector of the Parish of Stibbington. East of the Elton Road the remaining tunnel land belonged to the Duke of Bedford. Although at that time freehold land included the sky above and the land below to the centre of the Earth, the Agreement showed that both landowners were *"desirous of reserving to themselves the surface of the land over the said tunnel after the same shall have been completed... it hath therefore been agreed... that the same shall be reserved out of the sale and conveyance"*. Not only that but the *"ground and soil lying above the crown of the arch of the said tunnel and the freehold and inheritance thereof"* were also reserved by the landowners as were *"all the stone clay or other substance or soil that may be found in executing the (tunnel)"*. Thus while the L&BR had purchased land for the tunnel it did not own the surface and could not sell it back once the accommodation works were completed, nor was the company free, as had been anticipated, to use materials excavated from the tunnel.

The Agreement specifies that the L&BR could proceed with *"the construction and maintenance of a tunnel of the clear height of thirty feet and of the clear width of twenty four feet when completed with the walls and other works connected therewith"*. As the tunnel's diameter and in particular its height were larger than that necessary for the safe passage of trains, it is unclear if the height was specified by the land owners or was that intended by the company. The L&BR had *"full liberty to... open sink make and execute and from time to time and at all times hereinafter to maintain one permanent shaft of not exceeding ten feet in diameter and to also open sink and make such temporary shaft or shafts for and during the making and creating of the said tunnel as shall be required"* with proper fences having to be erected and maintained. The Agreement further states that the *"contractor shall be at liberty to occupy the surface land over the said Tunnel for the width of one chain or sixtysix feet for the purpose of laying and depositing thereon the soil which shall be excavated from the said Tunnel and the materials to be used in construction thereof"*. When work was completed the temporary shafts had to be filled and the surface made good.

The L&BR was also required to pay *"full compensation... for the permanent injury or damage that may have been done to the said land by such their occupation thereof"*. In this respect the two deeds mention different amounts though they do not simply relate to the same portion of land. Clearly the landowners were determined to achieve the most advantageous terms possible!

At the peak of the work the tunnel employed more than 1000 men. There were a number of accidents during construction, some of them fatal, but surprisingly there were no reported accidents as a result of the use of gunpowder. By 25th April, 1845 the tunnel was reported as being completed and open daily to visitors. While the Plan of Reference mentions a tunnel 688 yards long, as built the tunnel was 617 yards. Along each side of the tunnel there were six refuges spaced about 100 yards apart. Each tunnel end had a stone portal that at the Yarwell end being more ornate than that at the Wansford end. It had cost £7486 17s 0d.

Following the opening of the Nene Valley line the tunnel continued in use right up to line closure when it was still basically in good condition even though it was very wet in places and there had been some slight settlement over the years. From an LM&SR plan of February 1928 it is clear that the Wansford end of the tunnel and its cutting had a history of instability and there had been a large slip on the north side of the portal in the latr part of 1927 which was remedied.

In 1990 Wansford Tunnel was listed under Grade II as a building of special architectural or historic interest.

Chapter Five
CASTOR STATION

The history of Castor Station is obscure as it was one of the least important stations on the Northampton and Peterborough Railway. It was situated about 1 mile by road from the village of Castor and a ¼ mile less from the adjacent hamlet of Ailsworth, which it also served, but by foot the distance from Castor was less than a mile if a footpath across Normangate field was used. Castor Station was located 5¼ miles from Peterborough and 38¼ miles from Northampton Bridge Street.

Although the station's history might be obscure, a local railway plan for the time of building shows that land in this part of the Nene Valley was still being cultivated on the medieval strip system. When in 1842 surveyors acting for the L&BR were gathering information as to land ownership along the proposed branch line's route they probably faced their greatest challenge in the 2¾ mile section between Wansford and Alwalton. According to the Plan of Reference presented to Parliament, between the proposed Wansford and Lynch river bridges the line of the railway, including possible deviations, could potentially cross over 400 strips all individually owned. There were 50 strips in the hamlet of Sutton, 103 in Ailsworth and 273 in the Parish of Castor with 15 of the strips crossing the prospective trackbed in a one quarter mile length. The task facing the company's land agent was eased by many of the strips being owned by two major landowners. As a result this section required just ten deeds to record the purchase of some 158 strips from nine different owners. The deeds show that the Dean and Chapter of Peterborough Cathedral sold 64 strips, Earl Fitzwilliam 43 strips, the White family 18 strips and the Bishop of Peterborough, Rev George Butler, 8 strips. At the other extreme S T Wright of Castor and William Bate of Werrington each sold just one strip.

Once the N&PR Act had been obtained, Earl Fitzwilliam, who was opposed to the L&BR branch considering it to be *"manifestly absurd"* and favoured a rival line, was compelled to sell land in the area to the L&BR. Thus a deed dated 22nd July, 1844 conveyed 19½ acres of land *"situate, laying and being in the open and common fields of the Parish of Castor... and in the hamlets of Sutton and Ailsworth"* to the L&BR along with other land in the County of Northampton and an unidentified plot in Fletton for £5,690. As this sum was for all the land sold it is not possible to determine what was paid for the land at Castor nor the average price per acre. While some lesser landowners were only able to sell the exact amount of land the railway needed, it is clear that Fitzwilliam often compelled the L&BR to purchase whole strips even where only a small plot was required. Once the Nene Valley line was open Fitzwilliam was able to purchase back some unwanted plots, which he did around Castor Station in August 1853, though it is doubtful if he paid a price corresponding to his sale price. The L&BR and its successors retained some plots until sold to the Church Commissioners as recently as the 1950s.

Unlike Wansford and Overton, Castor was not an original Nene Valley line station but appears to have opened in about 1850, some five years after the opening of the railway in June 1845. Although the *Stamford Mercury* reported a minor incident at Castor Station in September 1848, a directory listing local stations, published the following year, made no mention of Castor. A possible explanation for this contradiction is that in its earliest years Castor was a semi-official halt and was probably unmanned. Castor appears in a Bradshaw's timetable of March 1850 and from then on timetables show that only slow trains were booked to call at Castor with most trains stopping only upon a request to the guard. In 1854 the journey from Peterborough took about twelve minutes and cost 1/- (5p) first class, 9d (4p) second class, and 5d (2p) parliamentary.

The layout of Castor station in its early years is unclear though a Station Master's house, on the right of the 1900 photograph, existed in 1851 and originally contained a small booking office which was closed when subsequent buildings on the Down side were improved. However, it is unknown if the other station buildings date from the early 1850s or the 1870s, a period when the growth in traffic using the line necessitated the extension or rebuilding of many of its stations. As the photograph shows, Castor consisted of two short brick platforms, approximately 210 ft in length, which were very low. The Station Master's house, situated very close to the line, was on the Up (Northampton) side, by the crossing to the west of which a pigsty and vegetable garden existed; staff certainly had the time to devote to these sidelines. The Up side had no shelter of any kind although a gents' urinal was

Castor Station looking towards Peterborough c1900. Photo: NVR Archives

positioned at track level at the Peterborough end of the platform. On the Down (Peterborough) side by the crossing was a brick building which was erected some time before 1897 but was extended in 1904. This had a bay window behind which was the station office and which held a ground frame whose five levers controlled the signals, one for each direction, and may have also worked the points into the station's only siding formed by a single spur on the north side. The siding had been added in September 1897 and its points, before 1904, had been operated by a ground frame elsewhere on the site. This building also contained the booking office with passengers having to obtain their tickets while standing outside under an awning. On the platform was a stage with an awning over the siding to enable a wagon to be loaded or unloaded in the dry and which contained a large oil lamp. Beyond this stage was a wooden general waiting room with a ladies' WC. The crossing gates were hand operated; road traffic could not have been great as to the south of the crossing the road was, and still is, little more than a field track. In latter days entry to the siding may have been electrically released from Wansford signal-box. The station yard contained a small weighbridge and associated office.

How close the Station Master's house was to the line is brought out from an LM&SR plan dated 10th April, 1931 following an accident at Castor. In the accident a guard by the name of Oliver was injured by the spouting on the house and although there are no other details of the accident it must be assumed that the guard was struck when he put his head out of a train window which would emphasise the limited clearance.

As traffic at Castor was never great, the only permanent member of staff was the Station Master, who was also booking clerk, crossing keeper, etc. Over the years Station Masters included Thomas Wright (1870s), John Green (1880s and in 1891), John Alfred Barnett (1890s), Lionel Green and Frank Abbot (1900s), Frederic Cowell (1910s) and Albert Edward Brooms in the 1920s. The 1881 Census returns show that Mr Green lived in the station house with his wife Mary, their daughter Gertrude who was listed as a scholar, and their two sons, Frederick W aged 14 and Lionel Anthony aged 16, both listed as porters. Lionel Anthony became Station Master in about 1903. During the 1926 General Strike Albert Brooms remained at work and received a certificate of thanks from the LM&SR. In 1954 Mr Hankin, the then Station Master at Castor, was succeeded by Albert Spicer who, as Station Master at Wansford, took on the responsibility for Castor and effectively became its last Station Master. If porters or other staff were required, they were supplied by Wansford when the need arose.

One of those who worked at Castor was Albert Spicer's wife who, after passing an examination, was appointed as its crossing keeper working a twelve-hour day with Jack Woodward covering the nights. To get between Wansford and Castor Mrs Spicer usually cycled beside the tracks but one winter's day she got stuck in a snow drift and managed to get a lift in the brake van of a passing goods train. On another occasion she set out by car from Wansford but was involved in a minor accident at Wansford crossroads. Despite pain she returned to the station and got a lift on a locomotive to Castor where she faced her twelve-hour turn of duty. There was a tragic event when Mrs Spicer, a qualified nurse, went to Castor station house to visit the mother of a railway family only to find her dead in bed. Deciding not to tell the children and with no outside telephone, she used the signal-post telephone to contact Wansford signal-box to have a message passed on to her husband.

Little goods traffic used Castor and as it had no cross-over the 'Up Goods' had to set back from Wansford. According to an LM&SR plan of the inter-war years, the railway still owned a large part of the field to the north of the station which was leased to Mr Rowland Longfoot of Home Farm, Castor in 1928. The LM&SR considered, but rejected, the provision of an additional siding and this was pencilled in on the plan. It is difficult, however, to see how the level of good traffic at Castor could have justified such an idea. In the 1950s the main customer was J W Taylor who took several wagons of coal a week while agricultural produce, including grain and seed potatoes, also passed through the station.

Castor Station had one known claim to fame which occurred during the Second World War. On the dark night of 3rd January, 1945 a V1 Flying Bomb exploded about 100 yards west of the level crossing at the end of some trees, immediately north of the line, the crater still being visible to this day. The 7.10 pm from Wansford passed over the area and stopped at Castor to report damage to the trackbed. The station was said to have been damaged by blast, though post war photographs do not show any signs of such damage, and the telephone wires from Wansford to Woodstone Wharf signal-box were cut. Mr P F Newell, the driver of a Down passenger train, was delayed at Wansford until the line was reported safe.

With the decline in passenger and goods traffic Castor Station closed to passengers on the 1st July, 1957 and with that its small booking office closed. In October 1960 the level crossing gates were set back to give the clearance from the track required at that time. The siding remained in use for a few more years, mainly for coal as it had few facilities for dealing with other traffic, with Castor finally closing to goods traffic on 28th December, 1964. Right to the end the station had no tap water while staff had to use earth closets. The station buildings and platforms had been demolished by 1965 and all that remains of the old station are the foundations of a brick hut in the yard, a loading gauge and a line of bricks which marked the Down platform. On the south side to the west of the crossing a pump is hidden in the long grass and bushes, all that remains of Mr Hankin's carefully cultivated lineside garden.

Castor Station buildings and level crossing from approach road 1950.   **Photo: Rev R Paten**

Chapter Six
OVERTON/ORTON WATERVILLE

Overton Station, to use its original name, was situated 2½ miles west of Peterborough, 39½ miles from Northampton and about 1 mile and ½ mile respectively from the villages of Orton Longueville and Orton Waterville. It was located in the Parish of Orton Longueville. The name Overton was an early form for Orton although the 1843 Act authorising the L&BR to build its branch line to Peterborough refers to the Parishes of Overton Longville and Overton Waterville in relation to properties and their owners along the proposed railway route. The station opened to passengers along with the other original stations on the Northampton and Peterborough Railway. It was a modest type of station serving an area where the combined population of the Ortons in 1851 only amounted to 526 inhabitants. The station was located where the railway crossed Ham Lane, then a private toll road but now the main access to Ferry Meadows County Park, which ran from the Ortons to Milton Hall, the seat of Earl Fitzwilliam.

Regarding land in the area, from various deeds it is apparent that the largest single purchase of land between Yarwell and Peterborough was the acquisition of some 16¼ acres of land, in various parcels, some two miles in length east from Ham Lane to the boundary between the Parishes of Orton Longueville and Woodstone. This land was purchased from Donald Lindsay trustee for the estate of the late Marquis of Huntly whose local residence was Orton Hall, now a hotel, and Charles Earl of Aboyne for £1195 4s 5d, about £75 per acre.

Between the site of the Lynch River Bridge and Ham Lane there were two land purchases. The Dean and Chapter of Peterborough Cathedral sold just under 11 acres of land from the river to the boundary between the Parishes of Alwalton and Orton Waterville, east of Alwalton Castle – now a riding centre, for £51 2s 3d, a mere £4 10s 0d per acre. Why a powerful body such as the Church accepted this low price is a mystery as there is no reason to believe that the land itself was of little agricultural value. In direct contrast the next parcel of land up to Ham Lane, amounting to some 2½ acres, belonging to Pembroke College, Cambridge, cost the railway £200 with an additional £200 for unspecified compensation. East of Ham Lane two separate plots of land which totalled some 3½ acres and formed part of the station site were purchased from the Rev Samuel Rogers, Rector of Orton Longueville, for £460. A further plot of land, less than a quarter of an acre, was obtained from the Rev John Mills, Rector of Orton Waterville for just £12!

The *Illustrated London News* of 14th June, 1845 carried an illustration of a railway policeman giving a hand signal of all clear to the driver of a Peterborough train in Lynch Cutting. On the opposite (north) side of the cutting the illustration also showed three posts which could well have been telegraph poles. It has been suggested that there was a private halt built for Earl Fitzwilliam near Lynch Bridge, half a mile to the west of Overton Station. The existence of such a halt is doubtful

A Northampton-Peterborough train receives the 'all clear' from a Railway Policeman in Lynch Cutting 1845.
Illustrated London News/Peterborough Museum

and would have been unnecessary as Ham Lane, which passed the station, led direct to Milton Hall. It is unclear if any special facilities were provided at the station for the exclusive use of the Earl although it is known that his family frequently used the station and was able to demand a special train. According to the *Stamford Mercury* for 20th June, 1845, soon after the line opened Earl Fitzwilliam was provided with a special train to take his family to London. As the Nene Valley line was single track at that time, the Fitzwilliam's train delayed the ordinary services. The illustration reveals that the original track must have been what became the Up (Northampton) line. It was therefore the Down (Peterborough) line that was added through Overton Station when the line was doubled in 1846 with the Down platform then being added.

Although Earl Fitzwilliam may not have had a private halt in Lynch Cutting, he did cause the L&BR to erect a bridge over the cutting which can be seen in the illustration. In March 1844 the Earl threatened to seek an injunction against the railway if it were to proceed with a level crossing at Alwalton. An estimate was therefore prepared to establish the cost of erecting a bridge near Alwalton to take the Fitzwilliam's private carriage road over the railway and of diverting the road. The Earl assented to this solution but at the end of October requested that the bridge be completed as soon as practicable though it is not known when it was finished. The cast iron bridge was supported on either side of the track by stone piers with the iron work being cast by Barwell Foundry in Northampton, Mr Barwell being the Mayor of that town. The Plan of Reference shows a track going from north to south, probably from Milton Ferry to Alwalton village, which ran through a wooded area beside the river (Alwalton Lynch) and this was most likely the private carriage road. It is known that this was a low bridge from the beginning as on the first public day those on the roof had to be made to stoop as a train went under the bridges between Peterborough and Wansford.

In 1845 three Up trains (to Northampton) and three Down trains (to Peterborough) called at the station each weekday, with one train each way on Sundays. Trains were allowed three minutes to reach Overton from Peterborough (surely a misprint as the journey must have taken longer) but about ten minutes from Overton to Peterborough to allow for a stop at the ticket platform, just short of Peterborough Station. In 1854 the fare to Peterborough was 1/- (5p) first class, 6d (2½p) second class and 2½d (1p) parliamentary. The number of passengers using Overton could never have been great serving as it did such few inhabitants.

An indication of what the early layout of the station was like can be obtained from a report made by Captain H W Tyler, Railway Inspector to the Board of Trade, following the explosion of a locomotive boiler on 30th May, 1864 while a train was at the station. In its early years the station appears to have consisted of little more than two short platforms, a Station Master's house and a hut for passengers. The alarming incident occurred to the 11.55 am fast passenger train from Peterborough for Northampton and London Euston, a through service being provided at that time, the train being hauled by a 15 year old Fairburn 2-2-2 locomotive No 297 built in 1849 for the South Staffordshire Railway but later acquired by the L&NWR and renumbered No 897. Although the express did not normally call at Overton, a special stop had been arranged for the benefit of *"...a pleasure party of 40 passengers..."* who may have been on their way to visit the Lynch or were guests of the Fitzwilliams. The boiler exploded just as the train was drawing to a halt in the Up platform. Fortunately the 100 passengers were unharmed, although the driver and fireman received some injuries. Tyler found that *"An open shed on the right of the engine was blown backwards into the hedge behind it and the booking office on the left was damaged, the ceiling having been blown down and the windows broken. The rails were undamaged but the ballast, which was only light, was blown away from under the engine"*.

As traffic along the railway steadily increased, improvements became necessary. In 1878 the *Peterborough Advertiser* reported that *"...the North Western Company has literally transformed its station at Overton. Readers will remember what a make shift it was, with one man to attend to everything. Now there is a siding for commercial traffic, a signal-box and signalman who, by approved machinery opens and closes the gates for the road which crosses the line on the level. Public conveniences have also been added and the little station made thoroughly respectable"*. This gives the impression that there had been no siding accommodation and that the signals and crossing gates must have been worked individually by hand. It has been confirmed that the signal-box, which was on the Down side to the east of the crossing, was opened some time in 1878 and most probably in February of that year. Its opening was almost certainly in connection with the conversion of the railway from operating under the permissive to the absolute block system which was completed by May 1878. In BR days the signal-box had a frame, marked '1898', with about 18 levers eight of which were used for signals and gates while others were for points and locks. This frame must have replaced the original one some time during or after that year. As at Wansford, the box had a brick base but timber top, part of the brick foundations still being visible to this day. The level

Overton Station looking towards Northampton c1900.   Photo: NVR Archives

crossing gates were operated by a large iron wheel. A photograph, which was probably taken before 1900, shows the station after the improvements of 1878 had been made as seen from the Up side looking towards Wansford. The crossing gates can be seen between the Station Master's office (the lower building being the ticket office) and the signal-box on the right. The wooden building by the name board was the passenger Waiting Room and there was a similar building on the opposite platform.

The improvements made in 1878 may have been needed to cope with an increase in the number of trippers using Overton Station on their way to Alwalton Lynch, a famous local beauty spot. Crowds of Victorian, and later Edwardian, Peterborians on Bank Holidays used to walk across the fields from the station to the Lynch to fish or picnic. It might also have been anticipated that the station would see an increase in traffic once the Yarwell Junction-Seaton link opened the following year and with the eventual opening of the GNR's Fletton Loop which had been authorised in 1875.

According to a Conveyance dated 28th February, 1885 the L&NWR purchased from the Marquis of Huntly 3¼ acres of land for £100 to the south and east of the existing station for the purpose of erecting four railwaymen's cottages, which were never built, and constructing a goods yard. Notwithstanding the 1878 newspaper report mentioning *"...a siding for commercial traffic..."* the plan associated with the deed clearly shows that no such siding existed before 1885; indeed the company owned no land on which the siding could have been built.

The Marquis saw fit to add into the Conveyance the clause that the railway *"...at their own expense make and thereafter maintain a good and sufficient wall not less than five feet and the half of another foot in height from the ground line to divide the land intended to be hereby conveyed..."* Why the Marquis required the railway to provide an expensive and seemingly unnecessary substantial brick wall to mark the land boundary rather than the traditional railway wood or post and wire fence is a mystery. As the wall was at the base of an embankment on which the station and its yard stood, the wall could not possibly screen the railway from his property. The wall can still be seen and is unusual in that it is a cavity wall made with bricks of a size standard to the L&NWR, namely 9 in x $4^{1/4}$ in x $3^{1/8}$ in. These were laid alternately as headers and stretchers though each brick was effectively laid on its side thus producing the cavity which was nearly 3 in.

For the first thirty years of its existence there was only one member of staff at Overton this being the Station Master, Henry Hughes, although the 1871 Census showed that he was assisted by Henry Crick, a Porter. The 1881 Census revealed that Joseph W Harris, aged 58, was then Station Master and he lived in the station house with his wife Mary. There were also two signalmen, Levi Wilson, aged 34, and John Turnwell, aged 58. A number of drivers lived in the Ortons who probably used the station when travelling to and from Peterborough. Local directories show that the Station Masters in the latter part of the century were John Howard in 1887, Philip Hunt in about 1884, Frederick Green in about 1898, and Henry Mayes in the early 1900s. However, the Census of 1891 did not show the current Station Master. In this century Arthur Davidson was Station Master in about 1910, William Hanks from about 1914 until the early 1920s, and A Gordon in about 1924.

In August 1913 the name of the station was changed to Orton Waterville, despite it still laying in the Parish of Orton Longueville, in order to avoid confusion and misdirection of goods between itself and stations with the same or a similar name. These included Overton on the London and South Western Railway, Overtown on the Caledonian Railway and Overton-on-Dee on the Cambrian Railway. A distinguished passenger who used the station about this time was C J Bowen Cooke who had become Chief Mechanical Engineer of the L&NWR in 1909 and had been born and was brought up at Orton Longueville Vicarage.

Old plans of Orton Waterville have been located and these include the L&NWR plan of 20th April, 1921 but redrawn with corrections on 5th September, 1953, a plan of the wharfs *c* 1930 and a plan of the Down platform Waiting Room dated 30th April, 1940. According to the plans, the station platforms were short, only about 180 ft long. On the Up side by the level crossing was the station house with a rear kitchen and adjacent Booking Office, the latter measuring 12 ft 3 in square. Beside the station house was a foot crossing to the Down platform which was backed by a small timber goods shed 16 ft 8 in square by 6 ft high mounted on a timber frame. Fruther along was a Ladies' Waiting Room, of the same dimensions as the goods shed, and a weighing machine. At the east end of both platforms was a gents' urinal. On the Down side was the signal-box by the crossing. The Down platform in about 1900 could only boast a wooden shelter but at some later date a proper enclosed wooden Waiting Room, with stove, canopy over the door and a large oil lamp on the external door, was added, the building being 20 ft long and 8 ft 4 in wide. The 1940 plan contained a proposal to move the Waiting Room to Carpenders Park on the LM&SR main line south of Watford Junction.

The 1921 plan shows that goods accommodation consisted of a single siding, with an adjoining roadway for carts, on the Up side, opened some time after 1885, which could only be approached off a trailing cross-over from the Down line which crossed the Up line by a diamond crossing just beyong the platform. This siding had a short 'V' spur at its end, one arm going to a carriage dock while the other arm went to the horse dock and coal wharfs. The goods accommodation was subsequently extended, possibly in the 1930s, by adding a trailing connection from the Up line, just east of the Up platform, into the existing siding and providing an additional siding by extending the existing siding through a set of points eastwards beyond the link into the Down line. The points appear to have been removed before 1953 but they did provide an indirect connection between the Up and Down lines. The carriage dock of the original siding may have been provided with Earl Fitzwilliam in mind. Before the First World War and possibly for a time afterwards, the Fitzwilliam Hunt regularly used the station. In the days before suitable road transport horses and hounds travelled by rail to the Leicestershire Hunts by special train so that riders and animals could arrive in tip top condition. Hound boxes were regularly stabled at Overton not only then but in later years. In the 1930s the main goods traffic was coal with occasional deliveries of grain, fertilizer and timber, the coal wharfs then belonging to Beasley and Son and The Peterborough Coal Association. By the yard entrance was an office and weighbridge (the building still exists) and on the south boundary a permanent way stacking ground. By this boundary was also the Station Master's chicken run, vegetable garden and orchard. The water supply came from a well to the west of the level crossing on the Up side although by the 1940s this had been condemned for drinking purposes and drinking water was delivered in churns by train.

In 1926 this otherwise insignificant country station probably achieved its only claim to fame, apart from the locomotive boiler explosion in 1864, when it won a plaque for the best kept station garden on the LM&SR which plaque still hung in the signal-box many years later.

Orton Waterville in the 1920s and 1930s began to feel the effects of road competition. From November 1933 to October 1937 Michael Smith was the combined Station Master, signalman, booking clerk and ticket inspector while his wife was the crossing keeper. All tickets had to be examined on trains to Peterborough as the station was the last outpost on what was by then the Western Division of the LM&SR. Between 1939 and 1960 Sidney Harbour and his wife Maggie looked after the station while living in the station house and brought up five children there. Mr Harbour worked during the day as Signalman in Orton Waterville signal-box during the first years of their being at the station while Maggie looked after the crossing between 4.30 pm and 8.00 am. Mrs Harbour worked seven days a week though there were some Sundays when there were no trains. The summer, especially at harvest, was the busiest time for her with farmers having fields on the north side of the line being regularly back and forth with tractors, cows and sheep. Even at this time the Fitzwilliam Hunt were still regular users of the crossing. Every time Mrs Harbour had to open the gates she had to leave the station house and cross the lines, and then operate the signals and the four crossing gates from the signal-box. Although there were Relief Signalmen to cover the nights and the annual holiday there were no Relief Crossing Keepers save for the annual holiday. One of the Harbour's daughters, Violet, recalls that even in her parents' day at the station there was no mains water or, initially, electricity supply. Water was obtained from the well from which it was pumped by hand into two large tanks situated on the upper side of the station house.

During the Second World War, in common with elsewhere, the name was removed from the signal-box. As one of the letters was lost, when the name was replaced it had one letter of a smaller size! Passenger services were withdrawn from Orton Waterville on 5th October, 1942. However, freight services continued while after D-Day in 1944 German POWs (prisoners of war) disembarked under armed escort on their way to Orton Hall POW Camp. At Christmas time local people were asked to take a POW for meals with two going to the station house and becoming regular visitors. During the hard winter of 1947 the POWs were used to dig out an engine and snow plough stuck in high drifts near the Lynch Bridge. Apart from coal, the agent for which in 1960 was Mr A Reedman, coal merchant of Chesterton, the freight consisted mainly of fertilizer, grain and timber.

The last Station Master was Albert Spicer who as Wansford's Station Master between 1954 and 1961 became responsible for Orton Waterville amongst other stations. He recalled that one train a day still called at the station to deliver drinking water. Orton Waterville closed to freight traffic on 28th December, 1964, the same day as did Castor. The sidings appear to have been lifted and the buildings demolished in 1965 or later, though the platforms had already been cut back by 1965. The signal-box continued in use until passenger services to Rugby ceased in 1966. A BR operating notice for 3rd July, 1966 gave the following information: *"Orton Waterville. The signal-box together with the Down and Up starting signals are abolished. The level crossing gates have been chained and padlocked across the railway and worked in future by train men. Keys to the padlocks are kept in Peterborough East signal-box"*. The closure date for the signal-box is given as 13th June, 1966, a week after passenger services on the line ceased, and it was demolished in 1968. The neighbouring boxes at Wansford and Woodstone Wharf were now only opened when necessary until their closure.

With the railway being worked as a single line between Peterborugh East and Wansford from Sunday, 26th February, 1967 the Up and Down distant signals for the crossing at Orton Waterville now applied to the single line. The Nene Valley line had another of its royal associations in 1971 when the Royal Train was stabled overnight in the Lynch Cutting on 8th July. At the time of the line's closure by BR in 1972 only a permanent way hut and the crossing gates remained.

Birmingham-Clacton train headed by Cl 5MT No 44914 passes the closed Orton Waterville Station, 6th May, 1957. Photo: J E James

Chapter Seven
LONGVILLE JUNCTION

The story of Longville Junction is similar to that of Yarwell Junction in that it did not exist when the Northampton and Peterborough Railway was opened and was not installed until 37 years later. The site of the junction lies about 50 yards from the south bank of the River Nene and lay to the east of where the Nene Parkway road (A1260), which was opened in 1974, now crosses the Nene Valley. According to a L&NWR Working Timetable of February 1901 the junction lay 42 miles from Northampton (Bridge Street), 49½ miles from Rugby and 1⅝ miles from Peterborough (GE). Although most of the line was built on an ambankment to keep the track above the flood level of the river, at Longville Junction it entered a shallow cutting. As to the land on which the junction was built, this was part of the 16¼ acres purchased by the L&BR from Donald Lindsay, trustee, as related in the previous chapter on Overton.

It was in this area that Marie Antoinette Marchioness of Huntly watched the N&PR being built. The Marchioness studied botany, geology and zoology and was a great specimen collector recording her findings and other events in a detailed diary from 1844. In that year she made frequent visits to the railway under construction, which passed within sight of her home at Orton Hall, partly out of curiosity and partly to obtain specimens of fossils and rocks unearthed by the navvies. On 12th May Marie Antoinette recorded that she *"...walked by the old bank of the rivers to Bottle bridge where we inspected the excavations made by the railroad men. Bought specimens of iron ore [of which] they discovered a considerable quantity... and injunctions to the men to bring up to the hall anything curious they might find"*. (Bottle bridge must refer to the present Boltoph Bridge in Oundle Road.) Four days later she walked *"...to the railway and brought home a wild plant"*. The Marchioness must have witnessed great activity because the *Stamford Mercury* for 17th May, 1844 reported that *"...the railway works in the neighbourhood of Woodstone and Orton are now progressing with more eagerness than was shown a few weeks ago, a party of men being employed all night in addition to those working in the day time"*. She did not confine herself to this area as on the afternoon of 23rd May she went out by gig to various places west of Orton Hall and looked at the railway works. It is unfortunate that there is a gap in her diary between November 1844 and August 1845 as the opening of the N&PR goes unrecorded but once it was open her family made good use of its services.

Longville Junction was a product of railway politics. On 7th July, 1873 the GNR was authorised to construct a 1¾ mile double track loop line from Fletton Junction to join the Nene Valley line at Longville Junction. The loop left the GNR's main line at a north facing junction, traversed a curve of 15 chains radius but was then straight until it joined the L&NWR line by a curve of 20 chains radius. Originally there were plans, never implemented, for a south facing curve at Fletton Junction which would have allowed through running between the loop and Kings Cross. Fletton Loop was built to give the GNR access to Leicester (Belgrave Road) via part of the L&NWR's Nene Valley line and the Yarwell-Seaton link. The main contractor for the loop was a Mr Whiteley of Leeds. By February 1880 the land and structures were ready though the rails still had to be laid, the loop being completed and passed by a government inspector by June 1882. However, it was not until 2nd July, 1883 that the line was opened, without ceremony. Longville Junction consisted of a double slip with an additional cross-over from the L&NWR's Down to the Up line just west of the junction.

The original service comprised four passenger trains, of no more than three carriages, each way on weekdays between Peterborough and Leicester, the journey taking between 1½ and 1¾ hours. Even in its early years the service was found to be uneconomic and from 1st November, 1884 one train each way was withdrawn. From 16th October, 1883 the GNR ran a goods service between Peterborough and Market Harborough though there was little traffic and the service was never frequent. Before the First World War ironstone was carried from Northamptonshire quarries by trains travelling via the Fletton Loop and the GNR main line to Boston Docks for export to Germany. The Fletton Loop was used in December 1884 by L&NWR services diverted due to floods while it was also used at various times by specials and excursions between Northampton and Skegness. As an economy measure during the First World War one passenger service each way between Peterborough and Leicester was withdrawn in 1915; the rest followed on 31st March, 1916. Although this enabled the junction signal-box to close, the loop continued to be used by excursions, theatrical specials and freight.

Signalling and the points at the junction were controlled from a signal-box opened in 1880. It is possible that a signal cabin or ground frame may have existed before this date to allow contractors access to the loop unless materials arrived only from the Fletton Junction end. The GNR's Way and Works Committee on 30th March, 1882 reported that the L&NWR had erected the box using their signals and apparatus but pointing out that the GNR's own apparatus (Saxby and Farmer) would have been about £200 cheaper. The costs were £659 5s 4d for materials and wages and £705 11s 2d for the signals. On the 6th July of that year the L&NWR had reduced the amount to be paid by £114 8s 11d. It is not clear whether the GNR had to pay the whole or a part of these costs. Longville Junction signal-box was to the south west of the junction and is marked on an Ordnance Survey map of 1901 though it may have been a temporary structure as at some point a 22 lever frame box was opened on the north (river) side of the junction its location being confirmed by a 1926 LM&SR plan. Like that at Woodstone Wharf, the box probably had a timber top. According to a Railway Clearing House map the box was 1 mile 18 chains from Overton and 1 mile 22 chains from the end of the boundary between the L&NWR and GER, just west of Peterborough (GE) Station.

In February 1901 the signal-box was closed between 7.40 pm and 8.30 am on weekdays and 7.40 pm Saturday and 8.30 am Monday at weekends; clearly the loop had no traffic between those hours. It was permanently closed about 1916 though it survived boarded up for many years. After this the junction was controlled from a ground frame which was released from Woodstone Wharf signal-box.

The main traffic along the Fletton Loop, however, was bricks. The loop provided access for traffic from the Fletton and Yaxley brickyards, as well as for those yards which had sidings off the loop, to Northampton and the Midlands via the Nene Valley line as well as to East Anglia and North East London, an area of rapid suburban growth, via the GER. The GNR attempted to discourage use of the GER's route to the capital by fixing charges for the transfer of freight off the Fletton Loop at a high level. Brick traffic continued to use the loop until some time before 1929 when Longville Junction was isolated from the loop, this probably being brought about by the general depression and the resulting slump in house building. A plan dated 23rd January, 1929 showed that the double junction had been removed and a length of rails taken out from each line at this end of the loop with scotch blocks being fitted by the L&NER. The plan also showed that the first 100 yards of track east of the junction belonged to the LM&SR. The loop was then worked as an industrial siding from Fletton Junction. It is possible that Longville Junction may have been out of use before the line was actually severed as Percy Newell, a driver at Woodstone loco depot at that time, recalled seeing sleepers fixed across the tracks on the loop side of the junction during the late 1920s.

The Central Sugar Company opened its Peterborough factory on land between the Fletton Loop and the Nene Valley line in 1926. Its main sidings were connected to the Fletton Loop but in 1928 two further exchange sidings were connected to the Nene Valley line to the east of Longville Junction, their entrance being controlled from Woodston Wharf signal-box by a switch release. Although not shown on a LM&SR plan of 1925, there was a connection on the Sugar Company's site between the two sets of sidings.

During the Second World War, following the bombing of the Midlands and the South West, there was an increase in brick traffic. The two reversals necessary for L&NER trains to reach the Nene Valley line added to the already serious congestion through the stations. As a temporary measure wagons were shunted through what was by then the British Sugar Corporation's sidings from the Fletton Loop side to the LM&SR exchange sidings. Why Longville Junction was not reinstated is unclear. It was the really heavy post-war brick traffic which resulted in the reinstatement of Longville Junction in December 1947 when a trailing connection was made operated by a ground frame which was electrically released from Woodston Wharf signal-box. By 1953 two trains a day ran via the Fletton Loop from Yaxley of which one was bound for the London Midland and Western Regions while the other required a reversal before going on to East Anglia. Westbound brick trains off the Fletton Loop probably ceased in the late 1950s. Certainly by the early 1960s the connection was little used.

On Saturday, 25th August, 1962 the RCTS ran its 'Fernie Rail Tour' over branch lines in Northamptonshire, the tour train running via the Nene Valley line and the Fletton Loop to Peterborough North. Later in that year Longville Junction was once again disconnected. Following closure of the Nene Valley line by BR the track and ballast were lifted from just east of the junction through to Peterborough.

Chapter Eight
WOODSTONE

The area on the south bank of the River Nene to the west of the bridge carrying the former Midland Railway line across the river lies mainly in the Parish of Woodston but partly in the Parish of Fletton, the parish boundary coinciding with Culvert No 70 over a small stream. This area has had an association with railways which goes back virtually to the opening of the Northampton to Peterborough Railway, though this association has not always been appreciated and has tended to be overlooked being hidden behind the GNR's viaduct and the houses on Oundle Road. Although the current spelling of Woodston appears to have been adopted in the early part of this century, the previous spelling, and that used by the railway, was Woodstone and some maps even from the 1930s used this form for the name of the parish. Woodstone will therefore be the spelling used in this chapter.

Woodstone never had a railway station as such due to its proximity to the original Peterborough Station, later known as Peterborough East Station, though from some time prior to 1858 a platform was installed for the collection of tickets which replaced the original one located just to the west of Peterborough Station. This new ticket platform was built on land owned by the ECR on the north side of the Nene Valley line between a culvert at the east end of the later locomotive shed and the Midland line at Nene Junction. This ticket platform continued in use until some time before the late 1930s when corridor stock was introduced allowing tickets to be collected on the train.

It was in this area in October 1846 that the Midland Railway's line, initially only from Stamford, crossed the River Nene and formed a junction with the Nene Valley line. Signalling at the junction in those early days was relatively simple and a plan of about 1848 shows a signalman's box in the 'V' of the junction with two signals beside the junction, one for the Midland line and the other for the Nene Valley line, there being no over-run provision for either signal.

L&NWR COKE OVENS

Soon after the arrival of the Nene Valley line in the city in 1845 the L&BR erected coke ovens in the Woodstone area to the north of their line. These were built on land purchased from Earl Fitzwilliam who owned large parcels of land in this part of the Parish of Fletton between the river and the present Oundle Road. The ovens were certainly in operation by 1848 as the *Illustrated London News* for October 1848 contained an illustration of the flooding of the Fair Meadow and a large chimney is depicted just beyond the junction of what was by then the L&NWR and the Midland line. By 1850 the L&NWR had about fifty coke ovens in Peterborough, most being on this site. Coke was the fuel then burnt in steam locomotives and it was not until the introduction of the firebox brick arch that coal could be burnt

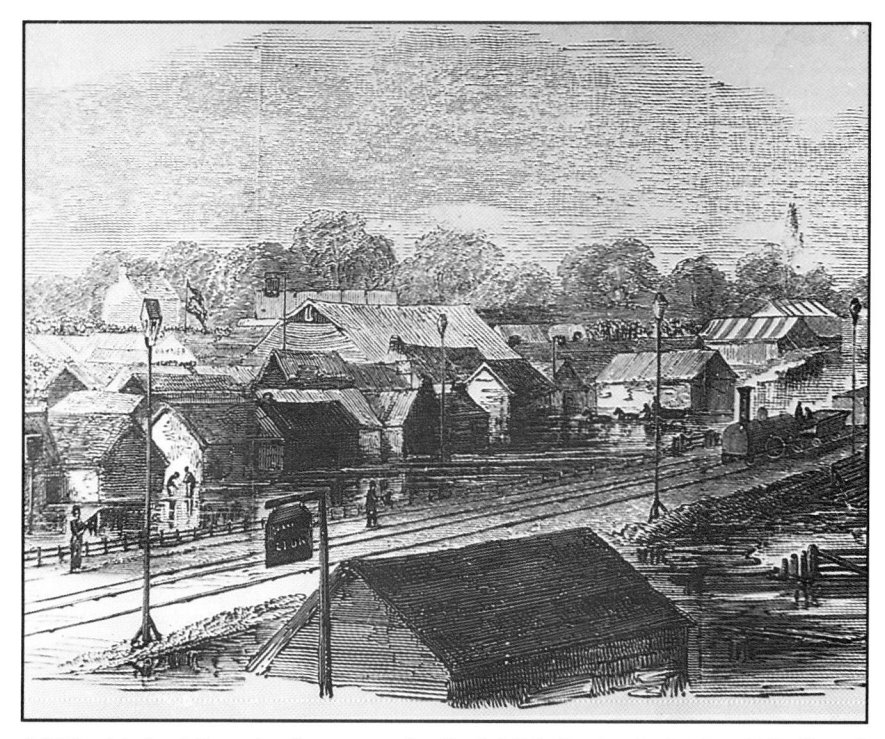

A Midland train at Nene Junction passes the flooded Fair Meadow in October 1848. The tall chimney of the L&NWR coke ovens can be seen on the right.

Illustrated London News/**Peterborough Museum**

efficiently. The Census of 1851 for the area included a coke oven house at which James Brown of Holborn, Middlesex, resided together with his wife and son, Brown's occupation being given as coke burner. An L&NWR plan shows that there was a cottage on the east side of a small inlet. Although an actual date is not known, it is believed that the coke ovens were closed some time before 1861 particularly as the 1861 Census does not list the cottage nor any occupants.

The coke ovens' site also contained a number of tanks sunk into the ground which were filled with water and served as quenching pits for the burning coke. What is thought to have been one of these tanks was discovered in May 1986, the rivetted iron tank being about 8 ft in diameter with its top covered by a metal sheet and a broken casting, the top having two circular openings one of which was plated over. About 4 ft down was a pipe which led off to the south. Despite there being sediment at the bottom, the tank was plumbed to a depth of 30 ft so that it could have had a capacity of about 9,300 gallons. Percy F Newell, who in 1919 started his railway career at the L&NWR loco shed (more of which later), knew of the tank and remembered, when young, asking some old drivers, who had started at the loco shed when it opened in 1885, about the tank. These drivers said that the tank had not been used as a water supply in their day but it dated from the old coke oven days confirming its probable use as a quenching pit. Apart from the tank discovered in 1986, the other tanks were probably filled in when the loco shed was built.

WOODSTONE WHARF

To the west of the Woodstone area is Wharf Road and beyond it, between the Nene Valley line trackbed and the river, is an area much of which is waste ground. Wharf Road, which runs from Oundle Road down to the line of the railway, is a reminder that a wharf was formerly present in this area. In fact a wharf existed in this area long before the arrival of the railway. Such a wharf can be traced back to mediaeval times when a royal charter was obtained for Yaxley market, goods for which were brought in by river via the wharf. Although river traffic declined in the face of railway competition, barges continued to ply up and down the Nene until well into the twentieth century.

For its line through the Parish of Woodstone the railway required a strip of land less than a quarter of a mile in length. According to the deeds, the L&BR purchased some 8½ acres of land from five different owners east of the Parish boundary between Orton Longueville and Woodstone for a total of £2,760, about £325 per acre. The most expensive plot, which lay immediately at the river end of Wharf Road and included the wharf area itself, was owned by one Samuel Burkle of Peterborough and cost £600 for just over a quarter of an acre. This did include two buildings which may have been connected with the old mediaeval wharf. William George Porter, a Peterborough surgeon, sold just over half an acre of land immediately west of the Parish Boundary between Woodstone and Fletton for £192.

Although F H Mair's *Traveller's Descriptive Guide* to the Nene Valley line published in 1846 makes no mention of Woodstone Wharf, the N&PR Committee Minutes for 11th June, 1846 reveal that an estimate from Mr Livock (who designed various stations on the Nene Valley line) was considered *"...for the proposed Wharf at Woodstone near Peterborough the amount being £1,299 16s 0d exclusive of rail and chairs"*. The Minutes also show that the Committee *"Ordered that the works be carried out by the Engineer at the Schedule of Prices furnished by Mr Brogden"* (who was the Contractor for the Oundle to Peterborough section of the Nene Valley line). These Minutes therefore suggest that Woodstone Wharf would have been provided in the second year following the opening of the line. As the estimated amount was a sizeable sum in those days, it must have included associated building(s) apart from the wharf. Land for the railway wharf was part of a five acre purchase, the Conveyance for which was dated 26th January, 1844. John Wray and others, and Thomas Wright sold the land which included room for the main line as well as a strip between it and the river beside, and to the west of Woodstone Staunch for £1,444, an average of £288 per acre. This investment in land in 1844, at an apparently inflated price compared with that of agricultural land purchased for other parts of the line, suggests that at a very early stage the need for rail/river transhipment facilities at Peterborough was recognized. As the Wray land was copyhold, as part of the transaction the company had to make a further payment to the Lord of the Manor of Woodstone of £11 8s 0d.

Woodstone Wharf was built immediately downstream of Woodstone Staunch between Culverts Nos 66 and 68, 1,078 yards west of the Peterborough Station. Although the wharf does not appear on an 1868 map of Peterborough, a railway goods shed does appear on a large scale Ordnance Survey map published in 1886 whose survey was carried out in the previous year. The description goods shed on the map was incorrect as the building was simply a wooden transfer shed of about 20 ft x 12 ft in size. There was no road access, the wharf being surrounded by marshland. The only land approach appears to have been via a footpath from Water Road, later Wharf Road, which crossed the tracks by Culvert No 67. In later years limited road access was possible under the low Wharf Road Bridge (No 68) which, being lower than the river, was subject to flooding and always very wet.

The original rail approach to the wharf was from the west off the Up (Northampton) line, no direct access being possible from the Down (Peterborough) line. A train from the Peterborough (Down) direction had to set back over a cross-over on to the wrong (Up) line and then pull forwards into the single siding into the wharf via a single diamond crossing. This approach was controlled by a ground frame which was probably located in a small hut marked on the 1886 map as being by the junction. Inside the wharf there were two sidings, one running through the transfer shed while the other ran just outside it with both terminating at wagon turnplates close to Culvert No 67. A single handcrane was located upstream of the shed beside the river. The map also shows the existence of a small landing stage by Wharf Road Bridge. The nearby Ferry Boat Inn suggests the existence of a ferry service over the river in pre-railway days and a row-boat ferry service was provided during the eighteenth century. With the growth in traffic along the Nene Valley line the use of ground frames to control access both to the wharf and the loco shed, subsequently built adjacent to the wharf, became unacceptable. As a

Woodstone Wharf signal-box and L&NWR DX Goods 0-6-0 loco viewed from the north bank of the River Nene c1900. Photo: Peterborough Museum

result Woodstone Wharf signal-box, with an 18 lever frame, was opened by 14th October, 1885. To avoid the need for two signal-boxes at Woodstone, a long siding linked the loco shed to the wharf enabling the original rail access to the wharf to be removed, a platelayer's hut being built over part of the original access trackbed adjacent the Down line by the former junction.

The wharf handled grain (the transfer shed was sometimes referred to as the grain shed), hay for the railway's shunting horses and straw for their stables. In the 1920s Mr Newell remembered that the long siding by the river was known to railwaymen as the hay or straw siding. Although following the arrival of the railways long distance traffic on the River Nene declined, short distance traffic may have increased as in the nineteenth century the Fens were better served by barges, which used the numerous drainage channels, than by road transport. It was often easier for Fen farmers to send produce by such barges to Peterborough for transfer to rail rather than attempt the shorter but more difficult overland route to the nearest railway station. This traffic continued until the early 1890s but then declined mainly due to the deterioration in the navigability of the Nene.

In March 1899 there was a serious fire. According to the *Peterborough Standard* four barges, the property of Mr Leverett of Woodstone who had recently started in business, were moored to several others alongside the wharf. The barges were loaded with 80 to 100 tons of pressed straw, the property of Messrs Keeble Bros, which was about to be transhipped into railway wagons. A high wind was blowing and it is probable that a spark from a locomotive passing on the Nene Valley line set the straw alight. There followed a comedy of errors. The man in charge of the wharf cut the barges free which, while saving the wharf, led to further problems. Three blazing barges and burning bales of straw, which had been thrown out from the barges, drifted downstream only to become lodged in the wooden supports of the old Midland Railway bridge thus placing the bridge in immediate danger. The fire brigade from the adjacent GNR's Sheet Department turned out and was supported by the Corporation and the Peterborough Volunteer Brigades. Men from the Midland Carriage & Wagon Departments and various Permanent Way gangs assisted. The absence of water hydrants caused problems and a lighter eventually had to be borrowed to tow the burning hulks away from the bridge, it being two hours before the situation was under control.

Besides the L&NWR's wharf in Peterborough, both the ECR and GNR had riverside wharfs in the city for the transfer of traffic between rail and river. In 1903 it appears that the various railways in Peterborough made the collective decision to abandon their previous system of rebates which had encouraged such transfer. The *Peterborough Standard* for 14th February, 1903 alerted its readers to a change in local railways' business methods at the end of April which could have the effect of doing away with the system of transhipping goods from water to rail. A report in the *Peterborough Advertiser* for 20th July, 1912 confirmed that the rebate of half-a-crown (12½p) per ton had been abandoned in 1903. Clearly the L&NWR and the other railways finally realised that the declining volume of transfer traffic no longer justified the continuation of the rebate; this decision effectively marked the termination of an involvement in river traffic on the Nene which had existed since the arrival of the railways nearly sixty years previously.

Despite the declining volume of transfer traffic, according to a plan dated 30th November, 1904 the old shed and associated engine house, office and weighbridge were to be demolished. A new modern grain shed was shown which would incorporate a canopy 150 ft long over the wharf to facilitate loading and unloading barges in the dry. Two tracks were to enter the shed with a third running under an awning on the south side of the building, all linked by wagon turnplates. The whole of the building was to be on piles to prevent flooding. With the minor alterations of there being only one track in the shed which was served by two hand cranes of five ton capacity, the new warehouse must have been built between 1903 and 1904. An L&NWR plan dated 13th January, 1922 shows a large warehouse 150 ft long and 30 ft wide with associated offices and gas engine house.

Woodstone Wharf and grain shed c1905.   Photo: Peterborough Museum

As no records survive relating to the volume of transfer traffic handled at Woodstone Wharf, it is not possible to follow its fortunes particularly during the First World War though there was little sign of any significant increase in Nene navigation at that time. What is known is that the LM&SR, which had absorbed the L&NWR at grouping, leased the wharf in 1923. This suggests that traffic must have been in decline for some years with the wharf possibly having been disused for a time. Certainly the GNR filled in their river basin on the north bank of the Nene in 1920 to make way for their Nene Carriage Sidings. In view of this, the L&NWR's 1922 plan may have been prepared to help decide on the wharf's future. The plan shows that a small section of track had been removed over Bridge 66A (a small culvert) and a buffer stop added to the adjacent points in such a position that made access impossible to the warehouse siding as this had originally formed part of the access road into the wharf. The fact that the culvert was not repaired immediately adds to the suggestion that the wharf was disused.

Woodstone Wharf was taken over by the Co-operative Wholesale Society in October 1923 for constructing its coal wagons and this will be dealt with below.

THE L&NWR LOCO SHED AT WOODSTONE

The L&NWR's first locomotive depot in Peterborough was close to the then Peterborough Station and what little is known about the depot is related in the chapter on that station. The opening of the Yarwell Junction-Seaton line produced a growth in traffic on the Nene Valley line increasing the pressure on the original loco depot. Thus the L&NWR required better facilities for their locomotives.

In August 1884, according to the L&NWR's records, F W Webb, the Railway's Chief Mechanical Engineer, *"...submitted a plan showing where the engine shed may be conveniently placed on the old coke oven ground near Peterborough Station"*. Approval was received *"...subject to the GER agreeing to reduce the rent charged at Peterborough by £150 per annum..."*, it no doubt being felt that the GER would benefit from the spare land created should the L&NWR move its shed. The new shed was thus built near Woodstone Staunch at a point opposite to the Peterborough Corporation bathing place – a location which was not appreciated by bathers!

The shed opened about September 1885 at a cost of between £4,000 and £5,000 and, according to a report in a local paper, it took about nine months to build. Due to its location beside the river, the underlying ground conditions were poor and extensive embankments one quarter of a mile long were required to raise the shed and tracks above flood level. Foundations of concrete, 8 ft thick, were required to support the shed which was of a standard straight type having six roads each over a pit of blue Staffordshire bricks. These roads were numbered 1 to 6 from right to left from the main line with No 6 being a short road. A further six pits were provided outside the shed although these may have been added later. There were three further sidings towards the river. The shed, which was of a functional design built in red brick, was 80 ft wide and 138 ft long with a northlight roof of slate and glass and was lit by 100 gas brackets. It was capable of holding twelve locomotives of its day. At the eastern end beyond the short No 6 road was a large sand furnace having an iron upper floor to store and dry sand which was attached to a shaft some 40 ft high. In this a fire was constantly kept burning in order to light an engine and so raise steam quickly in case of an emergency as well as drying the sand. At the same end were located the stores, a workshop, two offices and a messroom for enginemen, a cesspit being built by the messroom in the 1920s. On the river side was a coal stage over which was a large water tank measuring 37 ft by 32 ft and having a capacity of about 10,000 gallons. It was unlikely that water ever froze in the tank as it had a thick wood lining to prevfent this. In its early years the original well dug to provide water for the coke quenching pits was used as the water supply. In addition, by the river there was a 42 ft turntable.

A second ground frame, provided probably as a temporary measure for contractors, controlled the entrance to the shed but, as previously stated, the use of ground frames was considered unsatisfactory and it was replaced by the previously mentioned Woodstone Wharf signal-box.

The shed was reached by a footpath which ran from near the Cherry Tree public house on Oundle Road. Unlike the GNR, the L&NWR does not appear to have built houses for its servants and staff who lived instead in houses in the area adjacent to the shed, particularly in Jubilee Street, George Street, Grove Street and parts of Oundle Road. As the houses were close to the shed, wives often complained about smoke, especially on washing days.

Just south of the L&NWR line was a lodging house for enginemen, sometimes known as Cherry Tree House, which it is believed was built some time between 1891 and 1901 though the actual year is unknown. In later years the matron was Mrs Neale, the widow of a Rugby driver, it being L&NWR policy to help the wives of drivers who had died on duty. The lodge provided bed, boiling water and heat for loco crews whose turns prevented a return to their home shed at the end of their shift. The matron's first duty was to wake the crew for the 6.00 am Nuneaton empties, worked by Peterborough and Crewe men on alternate days, and her last was at 11.00 pm when she called the crew for the 1.15 am Aston goods.

The shed was a sub-shed of Rugby, as had the original shed been latterly, and it was given the Shed Code of 8P. Originally had an allocation of about 15 locomotives being between 10 and 15 in 1890. In the years before the First World War the shed still had an allocation of about 15 locomotives but was probably 14 in 1917. In 1919 the shed was still a Rugby sub-shed and had an allocation of 14 L&NWR locomotives consisting of:

5 ft 6 in 'Jumbos' Nos 253 *President Garfield,*
         394 *Eamont,*
         883 *Phantom,*
         890 *Sir Hardman Earle,*
         1170 *General,*
         1667 *Corunna,*
         1672 *Talavera,*
One DX goods No 3562,
C1 0-8-0s Nos 2555 and 2549,
One 17 in goods, and
Three 18 in goods.

Duties for the shed in the passenger link about this time were as follows:

6.55 am	All stations Peterborough to Northampton.
11.30 am	All stations Northampton to Peterborough.
8.10 am	All stations Peterborough to Rugby via Northampton.
10.50 am	All stations Peterborough to Market Harborough via Northampton and all stations Market Harborough to Peterborough via Northampton.
1.40 pm	All stations round trip Peterborough-Northampton-Market Harborough-Peterborough.
1.55 pm	All stations Peterborough to Rugby via Market Harborough and all stations Rugby to Peterborough via Market Harborough.
3.45 pm	All stations Peterborough to Nottingham Low Level via Northampton, Market Harborough and Welham Junction.
4.10 pm	All stations Peterborough to Rugby via Market Harborough.
9.00 pm	All stations Rugby to Peterborough via Market Harborough.

The crew of the 3.45 pm to Nottingham lodged at Netherfield and Colwick and returned by the same route before working the following night's:

9.00 pm	All stations Northampton to Peterborough.

Freight services were worked to Curzon Street (Birmingham), Leamington, Warwick, Nuneaton, Bescot, Northampton and Market Harborough.

Percy Newell, previously mentioned, started his working life at the loco shed on 28th July, 1919 and in his time at Woodstone the Loco Superintendent was Mr Nightingale and the Foremen were Messrs H J Bull, G Hayes and R W Hodson. Excluding Drivers, Firemen and Cleaners, the shed staff numbered about 20 comprising 3 Fitters together with their Mates, 3 Coalmen, 3 Boiler Washers, 3 Steamraisers, 3 Labourers, a Tuber and a Timekeeper/Storeman.

Mr Newell's starting pay was 8s (40p) a week plus £1 3s 0d (£1.15) War bonus. Being the youngest member of the staff for the first six months Percy was caller up, going round houses waking up staff. He also worked in the time office and dealt with the issue of stores but was soon transferred to become an engine cleaner. As there had been complaints regarding pollution, mainly oil and boiler scale, a large pipe had been laid in a culvert from behind the shed into the river and filled with porous bricks as a filter. Being small, Mr Newell was invariably detailed to change the bricks this being a filthy and muddy job the smell from which had an effect on his social life. By February 1923, aged 18, he became a passed cleaner being paid £2 2s 0d (£2.10) a week being eligible for firing duties if required. His first firing duty was on a train of empty coaching stock to Oundle for a special for boys from Oundle School. For instruction, Mr Newell attended the L&NWR Mutual Improvement Society held in the lodge, adjacent the shed. By 1930 he received £2 17s 0d (£2.85) a week or if firing £3 12s 0d (£3.60).

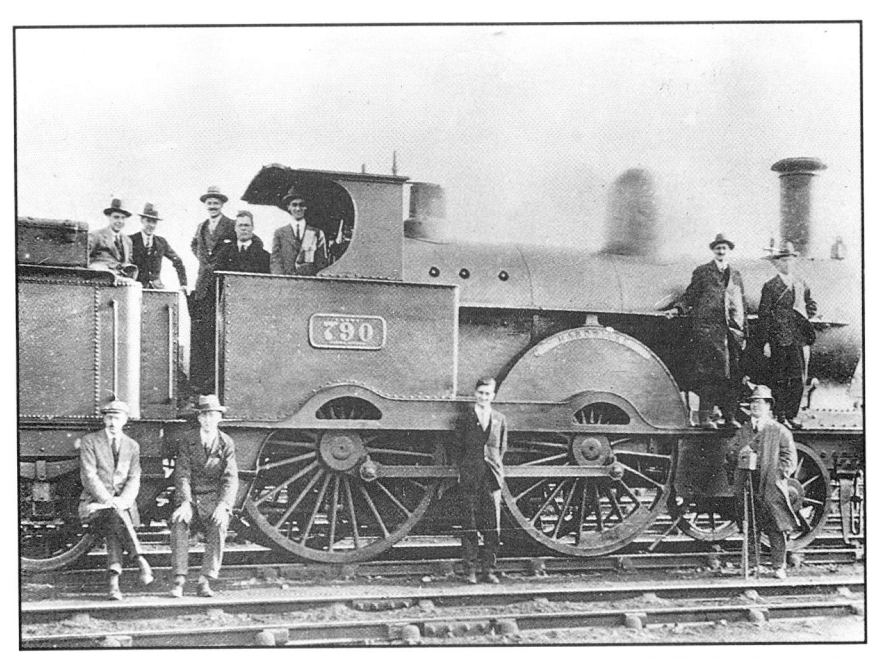

Members of the Stephenson Locomotive Society photographed with L&NWR No 790 *Hardwicke* during a visit to Woodstone loco shed in 1922 or 1923.   Photo: H M Lane/SLS

Woodstone loco shed staff in the late 1920s.   Photo: NVR Archives

After grouping in 1923, the shed was given the LM&SR Shed Code 9 and had an allocation of 15 locomotives. It then came under the LM&SR Midland Division and in its last years was a sub-shed of the former Midland Railway loco shed located near Spital Bridge which the LM&SR simply called Peterborough (16B). This resulted in Midland engines being seen on the former L&NWR shed. The small 42 ft 6 in turntable could just turn a 'Super D' but not an L&NWR 4-6-0 'Prince of Wales' class. To turn the latter, the tender had to be separated from the locomotive and turned first. On once occasion comeone forgot to apply the brake on the tender which ran away through buffer stops and ended up in a culvert! A worse situation occurred during the First World War when two coalmen, without proper authorisation and who were subsequently sacked, split a locomotive from its tender for turning which ended up with the loco running off the turntable into the river. Whenever possible large engines were turned at Spital Bridge or as previously, at Peterborough East though the LM&SR had to pay to use this turntable.

In the 1920s No 5031 *Hardwicke*, now part of the national collection, was a regular visitor having worked trains in from Northampton. A DX goods No 3537, which was vacuum fitted and had wooden brake blocks, was used for shunting around the shed and in the L&NWR yard at Peterborough East. Despite being beside the river the water supply at this time came from Braceborough but with a cheaper water rate at Seaton and Thrapston drivers were supposed to top up there whenever possible.

As it was uneconomic for the LM&SR to have two loco sheds in the city, the ex-L&NWR shed closed on 8th February, 1932. Just before closure the shed was apparently re-roofed at a cost of £1,000 though this did allow the building to survive for a third of a century after closure. The workings and the men were transferred to the ex-Midland shed where the arrival of foreigners caused much ill-feeling which lasted many years, especially as older Midland men found themselves junior to younger L&NWR men.

Following closure, the history of the shed is uncertain. For some years engines continued to use the shed, perhaps for storage. An aerial photograph taken by Aero Films on 19th July, 1932, five months after the shed's closure, showed the sidings being used to store old 6-wheel clerestory carriages. The turntable and watering facilities remained in use long after the official closure of the shed. Frank Waters, who started work on the LM&SR at Peterborough (16B) shed in May 1935, recalls his first Sunday job being to go to the former Woodstone shed with a gang of fitters to clean out the overhead water tank. Northampton shedded tank locos, which worked the Northampton-Peterborough services, were regularly turned and watered there which relieved the pressure on the facilities at Peterborough East. Passenger locos from Peterborough shed were also sent there for turning in 1940 when new pits and a turntable were being installed in the Midland round-house.

During the Second World War the loco shed was used as a government store and at one time is said to have been full of corned beef. For a time the CWS Wagon Works may have used the sidings for wagon storage. In the 1950s British Sugar Corporation wagons were stored there as were redundant bogie brick wagons while the shed itself may have held beet pulp. It seems that the yard ceased to be used by locomotives in 1953. Mitchells, the engineering firm, used the shed as a store in the early 1960s which was still standing in 1964. A BR temporary speed restrictions notice for the week commencing Saturday, 23rd January, 1965 showed that demolition of the wagon works, locomotive shed and removal of associated sidings were due in that week though did not take place until later. The shed was

Woodstone loco shed in 1964 before its demolition the following year. Photo: Barry Butler

demolished in April or May 1965 though afterwards some of its functions could still be discerned. The siding into the loco shed was removed by 14th November, 1965 while Woodstone Wharf signal-box was closed on 20th November, 1966 and subsequently demolished. The lodge was used in the late 1960s by the British Transport Police as their local headquarters and was not demolished until some time after 1972.

THE CWS WAGON WORKS

The CWS (Co-operative Wholesale Society) had outgrown its original wagon repair shop in the city which had opened in 1914 in a small cabin only 30 ft long by 20 ft wide. It was for this reason that the CWS took over the Woodstone Wharf for wagon building. According to the LM&SR Private Sidings Agreement signed on 9th November, 1923, the CWS had been in occupation since 29th September, the annual rent being £300 which was increased by £20 on 30th June, 1939. The Agreement stated that the LM&SR would deliver and collect wagons from the exchange siding while all internal shunting would be by CWS wagon capstans. As initially the CWS gas engine house was still incomplete and the capstans not yet connected up, the LM&SR agreed to shunt wagons as a temporary measure. The CWS appears to have taken advantage of this for in 1925 the LM&SR discovered that its engines were still shunting wagons in the sidings while CWS wagons were being held on the refuge siding nearest to the Nene Valley line, prohibited in the 1923 Agreement. At a meeting held on 27th February, 1925, the CWS claimed that its capstans were still not ready and the LM&SR agreed to shunt the sidings until 9th March. The refuge siding however was to be for the exclusive use of the LM&SR. It was also discovered at the meeting that new wagons were being sent by the LM&SR to the L&NER weighbridge in Peterborough for taring purposes free of charge; the L&NER subsequently charged 4d per wagon for the privilege.

No mention was made in the Agreement to the actual wharf. The CWS did not plan to use the river intending instead that everything should arrive and depart by rail. It is doubtful if barge traffic at the wharf resumed in 1923 and the CWS removed some of the timber staging in 1937. On Sundays when the works were normally closed, the wharf was used by boys to dive back into the river after swimming from the bathing station across the river!

When the CWS took over the premises, the interior of the shed was cleaned out and woodworking machinery installed. These machines were belt driven from overhead shafts connected to a gas engine. Alec Davis, who worked at the Wagon Works for 38 years from 1923, recalled that Harry Spinks was initially the Manager but was later succeeded by Sidney Cole, both hard task masters. Mr Cole would stand over an employee all day if he felt he was slacking but was fair to those who worked hard. Despite the Co-op having a good reputation as a kindly employer, working conditions were very rough and few stayed for long. Meals had to be taken where one worked and parts of the shed were very damp often with standing water which could freeze in winter. The working day was 10 hours while on Saturday work finished at dinner time; Sunday mornings were often worked in view of the poor pay. The CWS did not operate an apprenticeship scheme and trades were learnt by working as mate to experienced hands.

The CWS only dealt with its own wagons and had no dealings with other wagon works in the city. The works had a dual function, to repair cripples, perhaps those involved in an accident but which could still be moved by rail, and to build new coal wagons, orders for which came from all over the country. The 10-15 ton wagons were all to a standard design, but had detailed variations; there were side doors, end door tipplers, or bottom discharge wagons with a quick release lock.

The LM&SR trip shunter would deliver cripples or wagons of materials into the ready road, either during the night or early in the morning. After delivery the wagons were shunted into the shed or the internal sidings by means of a rope and capstan which could move five wagons at a time, wagons being turned, as necessary, on turntables. Wagons were next unloaded by hand, the oak for wagon frames coming from Miles, a Stamford dealer, with each timber bulk weighing about 5 cwt. Side panels of deal came from further afield while there were also wagons of the metal parts – wheel sets, axle boxes, buffers, draw gear, brake blocks, etc. It was all very heavy work.

Once the frame timbers of 16 ft x 12 in x 4 in had been marked out they were machined to shape, planed and mortised where necessary. The timbers were then moved by hand on to two heavy trestles for assembly. The side planks were added and retained in position with iron straps made by the blacksmith who had a power hammer to punch holes. The side doors were then cut out after which the wagon would be jacked up, wheels rolled under and associated gear added. Attaching the buffers was dangerous as it was necessary to fight against a 2 cwt coarse spring. Painting then followed. It took one man and his mate one week to assemble a wagon. Before leaving, a railway inspector would examine the wagon and it would then go for weighing to determine its tare weight. Once completed the order would be shunted in to the ready road for the trip shunter to collect.

In 1935 craftsmen at the CWS Works built a one-quarter scale model of their 12 ton coal wagon for display at Co-op fetes and exhibitions around the country. It was once displayed in the Peterborough Co-op but is now in the Museum of Science and

Industry in Manchester. A photograph of this wagon and of the Wagon Works staff in 1928 appeared in the *Evening Telegraph* on 5th September, 1980.

On 31st July, 1939 a new Lease was signed between the LM&SR and the CWS. The associated plan shows that by that date the main building had been further enlarged. A wagon traverser now gave access to three further sidings made of light section rail which, together with those previously present, provided sidings which could hold about 50 wagons.

The history of the CWS Works in the 1950s and 1960s has been traced through correspondence in the former BR private sidings file. A plan dated 8th November, 1950 shows that only minor additions had been made since 1939. In that year the main repair shop was a large steel-framed building with corrugated iron and asbestos cladding. In August 1950 the CWS obtained permission to demolish the old grain shed, which was life expired, and replace it with a modern steel structure. BR however complained about the poor state of the track in the sidings. The 1950s saw changes come slowly with elecricity installed and the arrival of a fork lift truck to ease manual labour. Steel wagons began to arrive for repair, usually involving rivetting, although it is uncertain if such wagons were built at the works.

In May 1963 the CWS gave formal notice of its intention to close its Works and to terminate its tenancy as from 25th December, 1963. Its main workshop was at that time 260 ft long and 72 ft wide. For a time BR tried to find a new tenant, the main problem being lack of proper road access. The situation was complicated by the proposal to single the Nene Valley line and remove sidings leading into the CWS Works. However, it was pointed out in December 1963 that *"...to date agreement for the singling has not been received from the Railways Board"*. It was realised that if the line was singled there would be room for a level crossing with road access, increasing the value of the site. The following month the replacement of Wharf Road Bridge by a level crossing was found not to be possible because *"...the present level of rail traffic is too high for the scheme to be adopted at the moment"*. Just how poor road access was to the site is shown by the difficulties the fire brigade had in attending a fire at the CWS Wagon Works just before they closed. The fire engines could get no further than Wharf Road Bridge where the dismounted fire pumps had to be man-handled under the railway bridge and along a compacted earth path to the wagon works. While it was proposed to single most of the Peterborough-Wansford line, the Woodstone Wharf to Peterborough East section would remain double track. It was also stated that *"...there are proposals to discontinue all passenger service over this route..."* although with regard to the Seaton service *"...it is likely that passenger trains will continue to run on that line throughout 1964"*. In view of the cost of repairing the track in the wharf sidings, BR decided not to press for rail use by the new tenant.

By April a manufacturer of structural steel work was considering a 21 year Lease of the site. It was anticipated that all the steel used would be delivered by rail and that the finished goods would be similarly dispatched with initial deliveries averaging 25 to 50 tons per week. The sidings would be served by the 7.15 am King's Cliffe trip working. The firm however required a guarantee that the sidings would continue to be rail served for the whole period of the Lease. BR could not give this guarantee although *"...whilst the level of traffic from the iron ore works at King's Cliffe and Nassington continues, the freight service will be maintained – there is no likelihood of the line being closed in the foreseeable future..."*.

Despite the assurance given by BR, no agreement was reached and the buildings were demolished probably about the same time as the loco shed with the track being taken up. Following closure of the Nene Valley line in 1972 the track and most of the ballast east of Longville Junction was subsequently removed.

Chapter Nine
PETERBOROUGH

It would have been expected that a company of the stature of the London and Birmingham Railway in building its branch from Blisworth Junction to Peterborough would have its own station in the city. That it originally intended to do so is quite clear from the Minutes of the Company and its Northampton and Peterborough Committee, and reports in local newspapers as will have been seen from the chapter entitled 'Countdown'. This chapter will consider the station that the Nene Valley line used in Peterborough mainly from the effect the station had on the line and its association with the line's successive operators.

That the site for a Peterborough station had been contemplated is apparent from a Northampton and Peterborough Committee meeting in March 1844 when a suggested alteration of the site was discussed and the Dean and Chapter, who owned most of the land involved, were reported to be in favour but Earl Fitzwilliam, having an interest in a small piece of land which was required, was opposed. The *Stamford Mercury* in that month also commented on the L&BR's wish for the station site to be within the bounds of the city, suggested Bates' Close as a favoured site and hoped that it could be accomplished without the assistance of Lord Fitzwilliam. The following month the *Mercury* first understood the station would be on premises of Pickney and Weston just over Peterborough Bridge with Earl Fitzwilliam having withdrawn his objections, then gave two other possible sites but in June confirmed that the Weston and Pickney premises (a variation on the name) had been finally settled on. Nothing more seems to have been reported on a station for Peterborough in that year except in July when Mr Bidder (the Contractor for the Oundle to Peterborough section of the line) undertook to confer with the Eastern Counties Railway regarding the proposed station and in September when an offer made by Messrs Core and Taverner to act as the Railway's Joint Agents at the station was accepted. Despite any further apparent action regarding Peteterborough, the Committee in September approved the plans and prices for other main stations along the line.

It is not until 26th February, 1845 that anything further arises regarding a Peterborough station for the Nene Valley line when Mr Bidder read to the Northampton and Peterborough Committee a resolution from the Northern and Eastern Railway Board. The resolution read *"That the Plans prepared by Mr (Robert) Stephenson for the Peterborough Station be submitted by him to the London and Birmingham Board for their approval, and when approved, that the Directors of this Company will proceed with the construction thereof, and will fix with that Board the rental to be paid by the London and Birmingham Committee for the use of the same Station"*. The Committee authorised Mr Stephenson to approve the Plans and requested him *"...to urge the immediate erection of the Station"*. Two days later the *Stamford Mercury* reported on preparations being made for the immediate erection of the station in the Horse Fairground at Peterborough which is thought to have been on the west side of Fletton Road.

Thus within just under a year the situation had changed from the L&BR contemplating having its own station to that of using the ECR's station. What could have triggered this change was the ECR obtained an Act on 4th July, 1844 to build their branch from Ely to Peterborough. As the ECR and the N&PR needed access to each other's line there seemed no point in duplicating facilities by each building its own station. The L&BR suggested the building of a joint station but the ECR would not agree and, as seen above, decided to build its own station which it allowed the L&BR to use. The N&PR built its line to its intended terminal point at the western edge of Fair Meadow, by Oundle Road, and the ECR managed to obtain permission from the Dean and Chapter to extend their line from the site for their station, across Fair Meadow to form an end-on junction with the Nene Valley line. This ownership division between the two companies and its successors remained until well into the days of railway nationalisation.

There are many who have thought that the first station in Peterborough had been built at the intended terminal point of the Nene Valley line with the names Cherry Tree (a nearby public house) or Wharf Road (mentioned in the previous chapter on Woodstone) being given for the station. The N&PR Act is cited as support for this, the Act authorising the line to terminate "*...near the city of Peterborough in a field... adjoining the turnpike road leading from Peterborough to Stilton*" while opposition from the Dean and Chapter, who owned Fair Meadow, appeared to be another factor why the station had to be built there. Further support for this view comes from a report in the *Stamford Mercury* in January 1843 giving the intended site for the station as being "*...near the Cherry Tree...*" and from the Chapter minutes in March recording no objection to the terminus being made "*...on the Western side of said Meadow, called the Fair Ground...*". In fact the need for such a station on this site was obviated by the arrangements made with the ECR but what compounded the view that a station actually existed on the site was the presence there for many years of a ticket platform with a ticket collector's hut. This ticket platform is mentioned in the previous chapter.

From the *Stamford Mercury* of 28th February, 1845 construction of the station could not have started until March and was hastened by the expected arrival of the Nene Valley line in May. On 9th May, 1845 that newspaper reported "*...one of two extraordinary large gates, crossing the line of railroad and the turnpike near the Crown at Fletton has been fixed during the last week*". In fact the line did not open until 2nd June at which time Peterborough Station was also opened; the events of the opening day are extensively covered in the chapter entitled 'Countdown'. According to the *Illustration London News*, Peterborough Station was then in "*...a very unfinished state...*", an illustration showing its west wing in detail and thus complete while the east side is in deep shadow. The style adopted for the station, which was more ornate than normally used by the ECR for their other stations, has led to speculation that the N&PR's architect was responsible for the design.

The station was built mainly on the site of buildings and a field owned by Charles Weston and Beata Pinchney (a further variation on the name) in the Parish of Fletton, thus confirming the report in the *Stamford Mercury* in June the previous year, but partly on land purchased from Earl Fitzwilliam. It was located on the eastern side of the main road from Stilton into the city near where the road crossed the river by a wooden bridge, the railway line into the station crossing the main road at Fletton level crossing. The station was as near to the city as was possible without crossing the river though its closeness to the river made it convenient for the transhipment of goods. By rail the station was $42\frac{1}{2}$ miles from Northampton and $47\frac{1}{2}$ miles from Blisworth Junction. As it was an open station and with the coaching stock then used not being corridor, passenger trains had to stop at a ticket platform right from the day of opening to allow passengers' tickets to be collected. Up to some time prior to 1858 this ticket platform was located between the Fletton level crossing and the station, after which it was moved to the Woodstone area as mentioned above and in the previous chapter. With traffic along the Nene Valley line substantially heavier than expected and the consequent doubling of the line, the station's facilities rapidly became inadequate.

Peterborough Station was connected to the electric telegraph which had been installed on the Nene Valley line and on the opening day a telegraph operator at Northampton asked his counterpart at Peterborough what the time was in that city. The telegraphed reply showed that there was a time difference of exactly five minutes between the two places, there being no standard time in England in those days with standard railway time not being adopted until 1852.

By September 1846 the station was said to contain "...*three breaths of roofing, extending over a space of 411 feet by 127, protect the platform and shelter the numerous engines and carriages which now appear to be continually traversing the large field of rails called the terminus*". A refreshment room and a waiting room with sleeping arrangements were then under construction. In front of the station, by the river, a large goods shed was being erected for the ECR. However, owing to insecure foundations, in November 1846 a large portion of the roof collapsed and had to be rebuilt. On 2nd October the Stamford to Peterborough section of the Midland Railway's Syston and Peterborough Railway opened bringing trains from Stamford into the Peterborough Station which were first worked by the L&NWR. The ECR's branch from Ely opened to passengers on 14th January, 1847, having opened to goods the previous month, making the above additions necessary. The ECR then worked the Stamford to Peterborough service. Peterborough now became a through station with the Ely line providing an alternative route to London to that via the Nene Valley line. Because of the nature of the station making connections between trains of the companies using it could have been better at times.

What may have been the first reported accident at Peterborough Station occurred on the 7th July, 1847 when the 2 o'clock passenger train from Stamford while entering the station rammed into a luggage train from Northampton which had arrived previously. As a result some of the luggage vans were crushed into splinters while there were some minor injuries. The cause of the accident was put down to the speed of the Stamford train but heavy rain had made the rails slippery. It was claimed that no signal had been given to stop the Stamford train and the *Stamford Mercury* for 15th October made the observation "...*it seems that the railway company have most regard to economy in the supply of attendants than is the preservation of life and limb for some of the porters disclosed that there was not sufficient assistance*". There appears to have been a general reduction of porters and gate keepers and a cut in their pay.

The missing portion of the Midland Railway's Syston and Peterborough Railway was completed in March 1848 and opened for passengers on 1st May bringing Midland trains to the station. On 17th October, 1848 the GNR's loop line to Lincoln, mentioned briefly in the Introduction, opened and brought further traffic to the station until August 1850 when its line from London was opened and which then used its own station in Peterborough. An 1848 site plan of the ECR station showed that the station had seven tracks under the arcading and two further south, there being separate arrival and departure sides with turnplates in between. Turnplates also provided the only access to the goods sheds. In those days of hand signalmen the signalling arrangements were very primitive.

In the meantime further building work had occurred in and around the station.

An 1849 local directory gave the following description of the site: *"At this station the trains run on one or the other of half a dozen sidings, and under a spacious iron roofing, supported by iron pillars, which form six avenues. The roofing is walled at each side; is of great height, 410 feet long and 228 feet wide. On both sides there are large stone platforms. There is a range of large brick buildings on the right, comprising refreshment and waiting rooms, booking offices, warehouses, engine houses, porters' lodges etc. The Eastern Counties Company enlarged it very much, built new warehouses, engine houses, and a large wharf close to the river, from which there are tramways to the main line, to facilitate the loading and unloading of goods. Close to the Station, ranges of houses, some three stories high, have been built for clerks and others. There is a handsome entrance to the Station, with stone pillars and iron gates; a constable's lodge is erected near it"*. At some time prior to 1865 the platform on the south side of the station was taken out and an island platform was added which was divided by a line for the transfer of small four wheel vehicles, carriages or wagons which together with others at each platform end went south into a large four road covered way. This covered way, an unusual feature of the station, was probably used to transfer goods though it did not have platforms. The positioning of the island platform, between the Up and Down lines, gave the Up line two platform faces. (At Peterborough the Up direction was that of Eastern Counties' trains to Ely and London.)

In 1862 the Eastern Counties Railway was one of the companies which formed the Great Eastern Railway following which the station became known as the Great Eastern Station being shown in timetables as Peterborough (GE).

For many years the L&NWR had a two-road locomotive shed at the station site and an 1865 plan of the site layout showed the shed to be at the east end of the station just north of the Up line and close to a six-road loco shed shared by the GER and the Midland. It is not certain who built or owned the shed. This shed was very small being about 150 ft long, probably built of wood and incorporated a tank house, it being likely that locomotives rarely gained access except for repair. Next to the shed was its own coke stage and small turntable, a water crane, engine pit and clearing house office. In August 1850 the shed came to the notice of the authorities in Crewe when *"...the men employed in the locomotive department at Peterborough applied for assistance towards erecting baths there..."* with Crewe's reply being *"...that the committee cannot sanction any outlay as the land does not belong to the company"*. The shed was at first independent being given the code '7' from January 1863 but was later a sub-shed of Rugby.

On various occasions the L&NWR considered building its own shed. In 1861 repairs were needed to the shed and it was recommended that a new shed should be built out of the materials of the already redundant coke ovens at Woodstone. The idea was rejected, the Company preferring to contribute £49 to the repair of the existing shed. The situation changed in the early 1880s with the opening of the Yarwell Junction-Seaton line towards the end of November 1879. This greatly increased the amount of traffic on the Nene Valley line requiring more locomotives to be allocated to the Peterborough shed which increased the pressure on its already inadequate facilities. As a result F W Webb received conditional approval for a plan to build a new locomotive shed on the site of the former coke ovens at Woodstone and the history of the new shed is related in the previous chapter.

At the west end of the station the L&NWR had a goods shed to the north of the Up line, one side of which was adjacent the approach road that led to the station. The shed had two large wooden doors facing the approach road and even at the end of their life the words 'LNWR Good Depot' could still be seen quite plainly in large painted letters; the L&NWR obviously used quality paint. In March 1845 the L&BR

offered to build a goods shed for Messrs Pickford & Co at Peterborough provided they took a 21 year lease. The following month Pickfords accepted the terms on the condition that the shed could be built to their plan. The layout plan of the site for 1848 shows two goods sheds to the west of the station divided by a wall with each shed being connected to the running lines by two tracks and a wagon turnplate though these turnplates were removed some time later.

From the opening of the station there had been complaints about the road approach. The incessant passage of horses, carriages and carts meant that in winter the approach was a sea of mud. Worse, as there was no defined path for pedestrians they were frequently in danger of being run down by speeding carts. It was not until 1880 that a proper curbed asphalt path, leading from the Crown Hotel to the main entrance, was laid. Over the entrance a glass awning was erected under which vehicles could discharge their passengers. In the same year the third class Ladies' and Gent's Waiting Rooms were converted into an enlarged Booking Office and Dispatch Office, the General Waiting Room was divided with a portion becoming a First Class Ladies' Waiting room and a new Smiths' bookstall was provided. The new Booking Office had three small windows marked 'GER', 'LNWR' and 'Midland Railway' respectively at each of which, in latter days, the same booking clerk could be seen, though not simultaneously!

A quarter of the station roof was demolished in August 1887 when a L&NWR goods engine shunted some wagons into the station at a higher than normal speed. The wagons, on entering the covered way, jumped the points and collided with the

Peterborough (GE) c1910. The L&NWR goods shed is on the left access being via the two wagon turnplates.
Photo: Michael Brooks Collection.

View of Peterborough (GE) from Fletton Road Junction signal-box c1910.
Photo: Michael Brooks Collection

iron columns supporting the roof on the south side. This demolished four bays on that side and the corresponding gable over the platforms on the other side. There were no injuries as at 4.20 am, when the accident occurred, there were few people around. With this being an appropriate time to rebuild the whole station, plans were subsequently made in 1896 for an extensive new station but were never implemented. The accident damage was never fully repaired and the whole of the covered way appears to have been removed probably soon after the accident. At some time between 1897 and 1901 the station was partly reconstructed with the platforms being lengthened and re-roofed. Many minor works were also carried out while the manner of working through the yard was altered. In 1917, in an attempt to reduce the unnecessary duplication of station facilities in the city, there was discussion regarding constructing a central station on the GNR's site, which L&NWR trains would reach via the Fletton Loop, and closing the Great Eastern station. Nothing came out of the discussions.

In 1918 E L Ahrons visited the station and his description of it cannot be bettered: *"From the outside the building looks like the relic of a Greek temple; inside the wayfarer finds two narrow, inconvenient platforms (one being an island), an assorted lot of pillars, a number of porters' barrows, and the main platform occupied by an empty London and North Western or sometimes a Midland train, sprawling the full length of that part of the station which is covered by a roof. These two railways act the part of the cuckoo at Peterborough, and do not give the Great Eastern bird much chance of seeing the interior of its own nest. The Great Eastern train by which the traveller wishes to depart stands patiently outside in the rain some distance away. Finally, there is such a generally dingy appearance that one gathers the impression that the station has not been touched up or renovated since the visit of the King of Mercia..."* Despite this state of affairs, the station remained basically unchanged until the withdrawal of passenger services.

Fletton level crossing had been a notorious bottle-neck ever since the station had opened. In 1848 the main road could be closed for more than a quarter of an hour at a time and with seventy trains using the crossing each day there was a call for a bridge. By 1855 the gates could be closed for 25 minutes at a time. The inconvenience increased further with the development of the brick industry and the southward spread of the city into Woodstone and Fletton, it being particularly bad at Fair times when crowds of people and nervous animals could be crushed together. Numerous petitions and protests over the years, including an appeal for a road tunnel in 1865, were ignored by the GER. A three-day survey in 1873 showed the gates were closed for a total of 13 hours 55 minutes to allow 765 trains to pass while a corresponding survey over a similar period in 1889 revealed that 1,883 trains passed over the crossing. A pedestrian footbridge was finally built by the GER in 1872, which was reconstructed in 1900, and in 1874 it was agreed that most shunting operations would be transferred to other yards. There were still long delays for traffic unable to use the footbridge and in January 1888 the *Peterborough Express* claimed it to be the second most dangerous crossing in England. This crossing required two gatemen for each turn of duty until it became wheel operated in 1920 and was in part responsible for confining Peterborough's tramway network to the north of the river.

Fletton Road level crossing in Spring 1934 just prior to the viaduct opening. The gates were controlled from the temporary gate cabin beside the footbridge. Photo: Madge Rimes

Although negotiations between the Great Eastern Railway and the local authorities for a new bridge were well advanced by 1913 the First World War caused the scheme to be dropped and it was not until 20th September, 1934 that the present road viaduct, spanning both the river and the railway, was opened. As a result The Crown public house, some cottages built by the GER and Fletton Road Junction signal-box, closed in May 1934, were demolished. The station was resignalled during the late 1920s and early 1930s with savings being made through amalgamation of signal-boxes and some remodelling of goods yards. Following the grouping of the railways in 1923 the station officially became known as Peterborough East which name it retained up to its closure. In April 1923 Peterborough East signal-box was opened, it being located on a gantry over the Up line at the west end of the station.

September 1960 Cl 4F 0-6-0 No 44519 departs from Peterborough East.   Photo: Barry Richardson

The 1959 BR Modernisation Plan proposed that Peterborough East Station should close and its days were obviously numbered. In 1963 the Beeching Report not only recommended the closure of the East Station but also of the Northampton and Rugby lines which they eventually did. About forty trains still called daily at the East Station in 1965 but with the closure of the Yarwell Junction to Seaton link in June 1966, Peterborough East finally closed to passengers though its last train was not along the Nene Valley line but to Liverpool Street.

The station was then converted into a parcels centre with the line between the main and island platforms being filled in at the west end and the general height of the platforms raised. Track alterations ensured that the main through lines avoided the platform roads. It now became the base for the East Anglian British Rail Universal Trolley Equipment (BRUTE) Service dealing daily with 15,000 parcels and continued in that role until 29th June, 1970 when the station finally became redundant and was subsequently demolished.

Chapter Ten

TRAINS ON THE LINE

Although this book is principally concerned with the various sites of the Northampton and Peterborough Railway between Yarwell and Peterborough, this chapter takes a very brief look at some of the trains that ran over the Nene Valley line. It is not intended to be a detailed study and some idea as to the level of services will have been gained already from the previous chapters.

Soon after the line opened there were five passenger trains along the line in each direction between Northampton and Peterborough on weekdays with the all-stations trains taking 2 hours while the faster trains took 1¾ hours. On Sundays there were just two trains in each direction, one slow and one fast. There was probably no great change in the level of service until 1879 when the opening of the Yarwell Junction-Seaton link brought additional trains along the line, as did the opening of the Fletton Loop four years later. As will have been seen from the Wansford chapter, in the 1880s twenty eight passenger trains to and from Peterborough stopped there on weekdays, it being likely that at that time all trains on the line stopped at Wansford. Before the First World War, one of the most important long distance trains which used the line was the Continental boat train to and from Harwich Parkstone Quay which ran via the Yarwell Junction-Seaton link. At some time during the war the advertised boat express was withdrawn as possibly were other services. These were restored in the 1920s when the level of service along the Northampton and Rugby lines differed little from that in the 1880s though the loss of the GNR's service via the Fletton Loop during the First World War meant that the number of weekday passenger trains along the line was down to twenty-two. By 1938 the number of trains had increased (thirty-eight were now stopping at Wansford) but following the start of the Second World War in 1939 the Harwich boat trains were withdrawn never to return to the Nene Valley line.

Following the war and nationalisation, services changed very little between 1951 and closure of the Northampton line in 1964 at the Peterborough end of the line. Between those years the Northampton line saw four trains on weekdays in the Peterborough direction and six in the Northampton direction, with extra trains in both directions on Saturdays. Most trains between Northampton and Peterborough were taking 1½ hours. The Rugby line carried around six trains on weekdays and extras on Saturdays in the Peterborough direction with a similar service in the Rugby direction. While the Northampton line did not carry trains on a Sunday the Rugby line had one train to Peterborough. The last train for Northampton left Peterborough East Station at 8.49 pm on 2nd May, 1964. It was a packed six coach train hauled by loco No 44837, with a laurel wreath on its smokebox, and was watched by a small crowd of mourners some with 'Down with Beeching' banners. The service on the Rugby line changed little in its last two years save that it lost its Sunday train in 1966.

The foregoing account only relates to passenger trains though the line carried goods services as well as various special workings over the years. These were particularly heavy during times of war with one such working being recalled by Percy Newell who, soon after the outbreak of the Second World War, drove a train-load of tanks, which were all manned, from Peterborough to Northampton. Other workings included football specials one of which, on Easter Monday, 1963, travelled from Swindon to Peterborough East via Northampton. This train was noteworthy in that it was hauled by BR Western class diesel hydraulic D1008 *Western Harrier*, this probably being the first time a Western Region main line hydraulic locomotive worked into the Peterborough area.

Royal Trains or their carriages seem to have made frequent appearances on the Nene Valley line even from early days. On Sunday, 4th July, 1847 two royal coaches, which had been built by the L&NWR, travelled over the Nene Valley line on their way to the ECR's London terminus at Shoreditch for use the following day to take the Royal Family to Cambridge. It is interesting to note that the only way to get these coaches from Euston to Shoreditch in 1847 was to send them via Northampton and Peterborough! Two years later Prince Albert returned to London via Peterborough and the Nene Valley line while in 1865, and again in 1874, there were reports of members of the Royal Family using the line to travel across country to get to their new residence at Sandringham. In later years the Royal Family used the Nene Valley line to visit the Duke of Gloucester after his purchase of Barnwell Manor in 1938. Some time prior to closure one of these trains is said to have been hauled by one of the Eastern Region's Deltic diesel locomotives.

One special working worth a mention took place in 1967. Mr R H N (Dick) Hardy, while he was Divisional Manager at Kings Cross, had the use of the General Manager's inspection coach to take his guests around his territory. On one occasion the guests included Sir John Betjeman and W O Bentley, who had been an apprentice at the GNR's Doncaster Locomotive Works and subsequently designed the Bentley motor cars, both being great lovers of railways. The journey that day took them to Peterborough and then on to what remained of the Nene Valley line as far as Oundle, this also being one of the limits of the Kings Cross Division's territory.

By 1969 the line was carrying very little traffic with a parcels train making a return run from Peterborough East to Oundle on Mondays and Thursdays, afternoons only. In addition, each weekday morning and afternoon, there was a return working from Whitemoor to Nassington Quarries to carry ironstone.

As for motive power, steam locomotives were employed on the Nene Valley line for practically the whole of its life with locos being supplied principally by Northampton, Rugby and the relevant Peterborough depot right into the 1950s. Until Peterborough Spital Bridge depot came under the control of BR's Eastern Region in 1950, the types of locomotives to be seen were mainly those from the LM&SR or its constituents, after which ex-L&NER types took over some of the services. In the 1960s steam gave way to diesel traction though steam did make a brief come-back in the early, and very bitter, months of 1963 when diesel locomotives were rendered unusable by their fuel freezing.

Chapter Eleven
PRESERVATION

Towards the end of the Introduction to this book the closure of the Nene Valley line by BR was seen as the end of one chapter in the line's history while another was about to begin. That further chapter was the preservation of that part of the line between Yarwell and the Woodston area of Peterborough as the Nene Valley Railway. It would be wrong to close this book without making a short reference to the NVR though, like many preserved railways, it justifies a book in itself.

The Peterborough Locomotive Society had in 1972 been established in the city for several years with its base for rolling stock at the British Sugar Corporation's sidings off the Fletton Loop. In March, following a change of name to the Peterborough Railway Society, it held a public meeting where the idea of the Nene Valley Railway was formally launched. Society officers co-operated with the Peterborough Development Corporation (PDC), and City and County Councils to produce a feasibility report which was published in June. This supported the establishment of a steam railway through the future Nene Park which was to be the leisure centre-piece of the new Greater Peterborough.

BR gave the Society permission to use Wansford signal-box, in which chickens had been kept, as its new base in April 1973. September saw the first items of stock arriving at Wansford and on 3rd November a Tenancy Agreement was signed with BR for the Wansford site excluding the old station building and yard. The PDC bought the Nene Valley line between Longville Junction and Yarwell Junction in March 1974 and leased it to the Society. The task now facing Society volunteers was enormous, especially with BR having neglected maintenance prior to closure. Two stations had been demolished while at Wansford, where the station building and yard had been sold for private use, there was just one short low platform and the signal-box. The line had no connection with BR nor to the Sugar Corporation's sidings, no passing loop and only a head-shunt for a siding; these all had to be rebuilt from scratch. Stock was able to move from the Sugar Corporation's sidings to Wansford following track laying which again connected Longville Junction to the Fletton Loop. Wansford Steam Centre opened for the 1974 Easter weekend though a steam shuttle service to Yarwell did not commence until the following year.

The initial idea was to use BR locomotives and stock though with the NVR arriving late on the scene, the only passenger locomotives available were rusting hulks from Barry Scrapyard in South Wales whose restoration would have been long and costly. Surplus BR carriages were also in short supply. The PDC, having paid out a considerable sum of money, were anxious that passenger services should commence as soon as possible and certainly before the opening of the Nene Park in 1978. The Society, which by then had one main line locomotive

(Richard Paten's 73050 *City of Peterborough*) and several small ex-industrial locomotives which were unsuitable to operate a 5½ mile service, faced a major problem. The Society was already providing a home for Richard Hurlock's Swedish Class S1 2-6-4T No 1928 when it was realised that foreign locos, especially those in excellent condition from a strategic reserve, could be an snswer to the NVR's problem and provide the unique spectacle of British and Continental locos and stock running alongside each other. Examination showed that with the demolition of one bridge plus platform alterations at Wansford the NVR could operate to Continental loading gauge. With Railway Inspectorate approval the NVR decided to operate to Berne gauge.

Between 1974 and 1977 the line was gradually upgraded to passenger standards. At Wansford the original platform was extended and track re-layed to link with that through platform 2, while signal and points were connected to an operating Wansford signal-box. As the station building was privately owned, Barnwell station building was acquired in 1977 and erected on platform 2. Just to the west of Longville Junction a run-round loop was installed at what became Orton Mere Station. In this period some British as well as Continental stock arrived on the railway. On 24th May, 1977 Major Rose, the Railway Inspector, inspected and passed the railway for passenger carrying operations and, following the grant of a Light Railway Order, the line between Wansford and Orton Mere was officially opened on 1st June. With the PDC aiming to open their Nene Park during the summer of 1978 a single platform station was opened on 17th May close to the site of the former Orton Waterville Station. In September 1978 Wansford turntable was commissioned, this having been removed from Peterborough East, and the following year the first stage of a loco shed was established at Wansford.

With no access of its own to Peterborough a Private Siding Agreement was signed with BR to allow a railway-chartered BR shuttle service to run over the Fletton Loop the first being in connection with the Eurosteam event in 1980. Although trains had ceased to run from Wansford to Yarwell in 1977 when the service to Orton Mere started, it had been the NVR's intention for trains to return there. Approval was given for a run-round loop at Yarwell, which opened on 17th September, 1983, and main train services were extended to Yarwell from 1984.

The railway's aim had always been to have a closer access to the centre of Peterborough than Orton Mere. With BR failing to sell the trackbed east of Longville Junction, by the early 1980s negotiations reopened with the PDC and agreement reached on the disposal of this land. The way was now clear for the NVR to consider plans for operating into Peterborough. Planning permission was obtained by the end of 1983 and in September 1984 track laying commenced. Following a Department of Transport inspection the first train to Peterborough Nene Valley Station, built close to the site of the old L&NWR Woodstone loco shed, ran on 24th May, 1986 with the Peterborough extension being officially opened by HRH Prince Edward on 30th June.

Following the opening to Peterborough the NVR has had time to turn to the less glamorous but no less vital tasks such as improvements in locomotive storage, improvements in trackwork to increase operating flexibility, and to the railway in general. New locomotives and rolling stock, both British and Continental, have continued to arrive over the years while a number of locomotives have made short-stay visits to the railway. The NVR has also been a popular location for television programmes and films, including the James Bond film 'Octopussy', as well as for many commercials.